REPEAL ROE. . . I TRIED.

By

Joseph E. Carlin

Copyright 2011

MR. JUSTICE REHNQUIST, dissenting.

"The Court's opinion brings to the decision of this troubling question both extensive historical fact and a wealth of legal scholarship. While the opinion thus commands my respect, I find myself nonetheless in fundamental disagreement with those parts of it that invalidate the Texas statute in question, and therefore dissent."

Roe V. Wade, Decided January 22, 1973.

TABLE OF CONTENTS

CHAPTER ONE   WHO AM I?

I guess my views on the sanctity of life started to form when I was about ten. Roe v. Wade was on the way to becoming law and it happened on January 22nd, 1973 when I was Twelve. But around the age of ten I was introduced to The Prayer to St. Joseph. I've said this prayer everyday since then.

It's easy to visualize the scene of a child in the arms of his father, a soft kiss on the head, a warm hug. It made me think. . . "what did that little kid ever do to anybody?" A baby is totally helpless, innocent and dependent on another person. That person may not always be a parent but let's face it, babies need love and care everyday. They can't survive without it.

I don't remember much about the Roe decision and it becoming law, just photos, memories of Right to Life campaigns, calls for trips to DC to protest, sermons at Church on Sunday. Over time, I think it became almost acceptable.

I am a Roman Catholic so my inherent belief lies in the sanctity of life. My personal views differ in that I believe a woman controls what grows on or in her body and if that just happens to be a human being, then greater care should be given before the decision is made to terminate the life. Consultations with the father, outreach programs that offer advice or counseling, religious contacts, family contact, adoption. After all that, if the woman decides to end the life then that is her decision, no one should be able to stand in her way.

I heard about the Unborn Victims of Violence Act on the evening news and that it was passed by one vote and it would be signed by President Bush as soon as possible. It also said this would give pro-life groups all the ammo they needed to overturn Roe v. Wade. I remember thinking to myself "Good, finally."

I heard the Act was signed into law on April 1st, 2004 by President George Bush. and that Sunday, April 4th, 2004, by chance, I attended Mass at one of several Churches I would attend Mass. This particular Sunday it was at St. Adalbert's here in Philadelphia. That Sunday, after Mass, a presentation was made of a relic from the soon to be Canonized St. Gianna Beretta Molla. This lady was devoted to her children and after a rough pregnancy, she went full term versus termination, against all advice of her physician. She passed away as a result of giving life to her new baby. She lived from 1922 until 1962 and was Canonized on May 16th, 2004 (30 days after I filed my suit) by Pope John Paul II.

I remember a woman spoke about what she considered a miracle when she had a healthy baby after being told she would have a very difficult pregnancy. She said during that time she prayed to St. Gianni, carried full term, the baby was born healthy..

What I heard on the news kept running through my head but all during the time after the Unborn Victims of Violence Act was made law, everything was silent. No one was doing anything. I thought pro-lifers would be standing on the court house steps, waiting for word the Act was now law, then file immediately to Repeal Roe v. Wade. No other news stories, no filings to overturn Roe v. Wade talk, nothing. I walked up to the alter and touched the glove, blessed myself and turned to leave. On the wall of the Church, off to my right, a framed picture of Pope John Paul II.

As I was walking back out of the Church I remember thinking, "Not me. You can't mean me. I'm not the one you want to do this, please." By the time I got to the door I had tears in my eyes. I knew I was called on, selected. Nothing I could do about it.

I realized I was holding myself out, ready to be branded by whoever I was going up against as someone who had no idea what I was doing, or knew what I was talking about, I was going to be made a joke of.

At Mass on Sunday we have a prayer we offer in the beginning where we ask for forgiveness "…for what I have done and what I have failed to do." This was something I had the knowledge of how to do and if I didn't do it, this would be something that fell under "what I have failed to do." I had the knowledge of how to file a lawsuit. I had the ways and means to do it. I had to find out why. Why was the Unborn Victim's of Violence Act exactly what the pro-life movement needed to overturn Roe v. Wade. I went home and went right to work.

The research begins. What I found was amazing.

Prayer to St. Joseph (over 1900 years old)

O St. Joseph whose protection is so great, so strong, so prompt before the Throne of God, I place in you all my interests and desires. O St. Joseph do assist me by your powerful intercession and obtain for me from your Divine Son all spiritual blessings through Jesus Christ, Our Lord; so that having engaged here below your Heavenly power I may offer my Thanksgiving and Homage to the most Loving of Fathers. O St. Joseph, I never weary contemplating you and Jesus asleep in your arms. I dare not approach while He reposes near your heart. Press him in my name and kiss His fine Head for me, and ask Him to return the Kiss when I draw my dying breath. St. Joseph , Patron of departing souls, pray for us. Amen

Say for nine consecutive mornings for anything you may desire. It has seldom been known to fail.

This prayer was found in the fiftieth year of Our Lord Jesus Christ. In 1500's it was sent by the Pope to Emperor Charles when he was going into battle.
Whoever reads this prayer or hears it or carries it, will never die a sudden death, nor be drowned, nor will poison take effect on them. They will not fall into the hands of the enemy nor be burned in any fire, nor will they be defeated in battle.

Prayer

God our Father, we praise You and we bless You
because in Saint Gianna Beretta Molla You have given
us one who witnessed to the Gospel as a young woman,
as a wife, as a mother and as a doctor.
We thank You because through the gift of her life we can
learn to welcome and honor every human person.

You, Lord Jesus, were for Gianna a splendid example.
She learned to recognize You in the beauty of nature. As
she was questioning her choice of vocation she went in
search of You and the best way to serve You. Through
her married love she became a sign of Your love for the
Church and for humanity. Like You, the Good
Samaritan, she cared for everyone who was sick, small
or weak. Following Your example, out of love she gave
herself entirely, generating new life.

Holy Spirit, Source of every perfection, give us wisdom,
intelligence and courage so that, following the example
of Saint Gianna and through her intercession, we may
know how to place ourselves at the service of each person
we meet in our personal, family and professional lives,
and thus grow in love and holiness. Amen.

Feast Day: April 28

Society of Saint Gianna
P.O. Box 59557
Philadelphia, PA 19102-9557
www.saintgianna.org

Saint Gianna Beretta Molla
1922-1962

Actual prayer card I received after touching the relic of the soon to be
Canonized Saint Gianna Beretta Molla

CHAPTER TWO   THE LAW

I started with a copy of the Law, Roe v. Wade. I don't know if many people had a chance to read this decision, I certainly had not before this, but here is a copy.

ROE v. WADE

Decided January 22, 1973

MR. JUSTICE BLACKMUN delivered the opinion of the Court.

MR. JUSTICE REHNQUIST, dissenting.

MR. JUSTICE STEWART, concurring.

A pregnant single woman (Roe) brought a class action challenging the constitutionality of the Texas criminal abortion laws, which proscribe procuring or attempting an abortion except on medical advice for the purpose of saving the mother's life. A licensed physician (Hallford), who had two state abortion prosecutions pending against him, was permitted to intervene. A childless married couple (the Does), the wife not being pregnant, separately attacked the laws, basing alleged injury on the future possibilities of contraceptive failure, pregnancy, unpreparedness for parenthood, and impairment of the wife's health. A three-judge District Court, which consolidated the actions, held that Roe and Hallford, and members of their classes, had standing to sue and presented justiciable controversies. Ruling that declaratory, though not injunctive, relief was warranted, the court declared the abortion statutes void as vague and overbroadly infringing those plaintiffs' Ninth and Fourteenth Amendment rights. The court ruled the Does' complaint not justiciable. Appellants directly appealed to this Court on the injunctive rulings, and appellee cross-appealed from the District Court's grant of declaratory relief to Roe and Hallford. Held:

1. While 28 U. S. C. § 1253 authorizes no direct appeal to this Court from the grant or denial of declaratory relief alone, review is not foreclosed when the case is properly before the Court on appeal from specific denial of injunctive relief and the arguments as to both injunctive and declaratory relief are necessarily identical. P. 123.

2. Roe has standing to sue; the Does and Hallford do not. Pp. 123-129.

(a) Contrary to appellee's contention, the natural termination of Roe's pregnancy did not moot her suit. Litigation involving pregnancy, which is "capable of repetition, yet evading review," is an exception to the usual federal rule that an actual controversy must exist at review stages and not simply when the action is initiated. Pp. 124-125.

(b) The District Court correctly refused injunctive, but erred in granting declaratory, relief to Hallford, who alleged no federally protected right not assertable as a defense against the good-faith state prosecutions pending against him. Samuels v. Mackell, 401 U.S. 66. Pp. 125-127.

(c) The Does' complaint, based as it is on contingencies, any one or more of which may not occur, is too speculative to present an actual case or controversy. Pp. 127-129.

3. State criminal abortion laws, like those involved here, that except from criminality only a lifesaving procedure on the mother's behalf without regard to the stage of her pregnancy and other interests involved violate the Due Process Clause of the Fourteenth Amendment, which protects against state action the right to privacy, including a woman's qualified right to terminate her pregnancy. Though the State cannot override that right, it has legitimate interests in protecting both the pregnant woman's health and the potentiality of human life, each of which interests grows and reaches a "compelling" point at various stages of the woman's approach to term. Pp. 147-164.

(a) For the stage prior to approximately the end of the first trimester, the abortion decision and its effectuation must be left to the medical judgment of the pregnant woman's attending physician. Pp. 163, 164.

(b) For the stage subsequent to approximately the end of the first trimester, the State, in promoting its interest in the health of the mother, may, if it chooses, regulate the abortion procedure in ways that are reasonably related to maternal health. Pp. 163, 164.

(c) For the stage subsequent to viability the State, in promoting its interest in the potentiality of human life, may, if it chooses, regulate, and even proscribe, abortion except where necessary, in appropriate medical judgment, for the preservation of the life or health of the mother. Pp. 163-164; 164-165.

4. The State may define the term "physician" to mean only a physician currently licensed by the State, and may proscribe any abortion by a person who is not a physician as so defined. P. 165.

5. It is unnecessary to decide the injunctive relief issue since the Texas authorities will doubtless fully recognize the Court's ruling that the Texas criminal abortion statutes are unconstitutional. P. 166.

MR. JUSTICE BLACKMUN delivered the opinion of the Court.

This Texas federal appeal and its Georgia companion, Doe v. Bolton, post, p. 179, present constitutional challenges to state criminal abortion legislation. The Texas statutes under attack here are typical of those that have been in effect in many States for approximately a century. The Georgia statutes, in contrast, have a modern cast and are a legislative product that, to an extent at least, obviously reflects the influences of recent attitudinal change, of advancing medical knowledge and techniques, and of new thinking about an old issue.

We forthwith acknowledge our awareness of the sensitive and emotional nature of the abortion controversy, of the vigorous opposing views, even among physicians, and of the deep and seemingly absolute convictions that the subject inspires. One's philosophy, one's experiences, one's exposure to the raw edges of human existence, one's religious training, one's attitudes toward life and family and their values, and the moral standards one establishes and seeks to observe, are all likely to influence and to color one's thinking and conclusions about abortion.

In addition, population growth, pollution, poverty, and racial overtones tend to complicate and not to simplify the problem.

Our task, of course, is to resolve the issue by constitutional measurement, free of emotion and of predilection. We seek earnestly to do this, and, because we do, we have inquired into, and in this opinion place some emphasis upon, medical and medical-legal history and what that history reveals about man's attitudes toward the abortion procedure over the centuries. We bear in mind, too, Mr. Justice Holmes' admonition in his now-vindicated dissent in Lochner v. New York, 198 U.S. 45, 76 (1905):

"[The Constitution] is made for people of fundamentally differing views, and the accident of our finding certain opinions natural and familiar or novel and even shocking ought not to conclude our judgment upon the question whether statutes embodying them conflict with the Constitution of the United States."

I

The Texas statutes that concern us here are Arts. 1191-1194 and 1196 of the State's Penal Code. [1] These make it a crime to "procure an abortion," as therein defined, or to attempt one, except with respect to "an abortion procured or attempted by medical advice for the purpose of saving the life of the mother." Similar statutes are in existence in a majority of the States. [2]

Texas first enacted a criminal abortion statute in 1854. Texas Laws 1854, c. 49, § 1, set forth in 3 H. Gammel, Laws of Texas 1502 (1898). This was soon modified into language that has remained substantially unchanged to the present time. See Texas Penal Code of 1857, c. 7, Arts. 531-536; G. Paschal, Laws of Texas, Arts. 2192-2197 (1866); Texas Rev. Stat., c. 8, Arts. 536-541 (1879); Texas Rev. Crim. Stat., Arts. 1071-1076 (1911). The final article in each of these compilations provided the same exception, as does the present Article 1196, for an abortion by "medical advice for the purpose of saving the life of the mother." [3]

II

Jane Roe, [4] a single woman who was residing in Dallas County, Texas, instituted this federal action in March 1970 against the District Attorney of the county. She sought a declaratory judgment that the Texas criminal abortion statutes were unconstitutional on their face, and an injunction restraining the defendant from enforcing the statutes.

Roe alleged that she was unmarried and pregnant; that she wished to terminate her pregnancy by an abortion "performed by a competent, licensed physician, under safe, clinical conditions"; that she was unable to get a "legal" abortion in Texas because her life did not appear to be threatened by the continuation of her pregnancy; and that she could not afford to travel to another jurisdiction in order to secure a legal abortion under safe conditions. She claimed that the Texas statutes were unconstitutionally vague and that they abridged her right of personal privacy, protected by the First, Fourth, Fifth, Ninth, and Fourteenth Amendments. By an amendment to her complaint Roe purported to sue "on behalf of herself and all other women" similarly situated.

James Hubert Hallford, a licensed physician, sought and was granted leave to intervene in Roe's action. In his complaint he alleged that he had been arrested previously for violations of the Texas abortion statutes and that two such prosecutions were pending against him. He described conditions of patients who came to him seeking abortions, and he claimed that for many cases he, as a physician, was unable to determine whether they fell within or outside the exception recognized by Article 1196. He alleged that, as a consequence, the statutes were vague and uncertain, in violation of the Fourteenth Amendment, and that they violated his own and his patients' rights to privacy in the doctor-patient relationship and his own right to practice medicine, rights he claimed were guaranteed by the First, Fourth, Fifth, Ninth, and Fourteenth Amendments.

John and Mary Doe, 5 a married couple, filed a companion complaint to that of Roe. They also named the District Attorney as defendant, claimed like constitutional deprivations, and sought declaratory and injunctive relief. The Does alleged that they were a childless couple; that Mrs. Doe was suffering from a "neural-chemical" disorder; that her physician had "advised her to avoid pregnancy until such time as her condition has materially improved" (although a pregnancy at the present time would not present "a serious risk" to her life); that, pursuant to medical advice, she had discontinued use of birth control pills; and that if she should become pregnant, she would want to terminate the pregnancy by an abortion performed by a competent, licensed physician under safe, clinical conditions. By an amendment to their complaint, the Does purported to sue "on behalf of themselves and all couples similarly situated."

The two actions were consolidated and heard together by a duly convened three-judge district court. The suits thus presented the situations of the pregnant single woman, the childless couple, with the wife not pregnant, and the licensed practicing physician, all joining in the attack on the Texas criminal abortion statutes. Upon the filing of affidavits, motions were made for dismissal and for summary judgment. The court held that Roe and members of her class, and Dr. Hallford, had standing to sue and presented justiciable controversies, but that the Does had failed to allege facts sufficient to state a present controversy and did not have standing. It concluded that, with respect to the requests for a declaratory judgment, abstention was not warranted. On the merits, the District Court held that the "fundamental right of single women and married persons to choose whether to have children is protected by the Ninth Amendment, through the Fourteenth Amendment," and that the Texas criminal abortion statutes were void on their face because they were both unconstitutionally vague and constituted an overbroad infringement of the plaintiffs' Ninth Amendment rights. The court then held that abstention was warranted with respect to the requests for an injunction. It therefore dismissed the Does' complaint, declared the abortion statutes void, and dismissed the application for injunctive relief. 314 F.Supp. 1217, 1225 (ND Tex. 1970).

The plaintiffs Roe and Doe and the intervenor Hallford, pursuant to 28 U. S. C. § 1253, have appealed to this Court from that part of the District Court's judgment denying the injunction. The defendant District Attorney has purported to cross-appeal, pursuant to the same statute, from the court's grant of declaratory relief to Roe and Hallford. Both sides also have taken protective appeals to the United States Court of Appeals for the Fifth Circuit. That court ordered the appeals held in abeyance pending decision here. We postponed decision on jurisdiction to the hearing on the merits. 402 U.S. 941 (1971).

III

It might have been preferable if the defendant, pursuant to our Rule 20, had presented to us a petition for certiorari before judgment in the Court of Appeals with respect to the granting of the plaintiffs' prayer for declaratory relief. Our decisions in Mitchell v. Donovan, 398 U.S. 427 (1970), and Gunn v. University Committee, 399 U.S. 383 (1970), are to the effect that § 1253 does not authorize an appeal to this Court from the grant or denial of declaratory relief alone. We conclude, nevertheless, that those decisions do not foreclose our review of both the injunctive and the declaratory aspects of a case of this kind when it is properly here, as this one is, on appeal under § 1253 from specific denial of injunctive relief, and the arguments as to both aspects are necessarily identical. See Carter v. Jury Comm'n, 396 U.S. 320 (1970); Florida Lime Growers v. Jacobsen, 362 U.S. 73, 80-81 (1960). It would be destructive of time and energy for all concerned were we to rule otherwise. Cf. Doe v. Bolton, post, p. 179.

IV

We are next confronted with issues of justiciability, standing, and abstention. Have Roe and the Does established that "personal stake in the outcome of the controversy," Baker v. Carr, 369 U.S. 186, 204 (1962), that insures that "the dispute sought to be adjudicated will be presented in an adversary context and in a form historically viewed as capable of judicial resolution," Flast v. Cohen, 392 U.S. 83, 101 (1968), and Sierra Club v. Morton, 405 U.S. 727, 732 (1972)? And what effect did the pendency of criminal abortion charges against Dr. Hallford in state court have upon the propriety of the federal court's granting relief to him as a plaintiff-intervenor? A. Jane Roe. Despite the use of the pseudonym, no suggestion is made that Roe is a fictitious person. For purposes of her case, we accept as true, and as established, her existence; her pregnant state, as of the inception of her suit in March 1970 and as late as May 21 of that year when she filed an alias affidavit with the District Court; and her inability to obtain a legal abortion in Texas.

Viewing Roe's case as of the time of its filing and thereafter until as late as May, there can be little dispute that it then presented a case or controversy and that, wholly apart from the class aspects, she, as a pregnant single woman thwarted by the Texas criminal abortion laws, had standing to challenge those statutes. Abele v. Markle, 452 F.2d 1121, 1125 (CA2 1971); Crossen v. Breckenridge, 446 F.2d 833, 838-839 (CA6 1971); Poe v. Menghini, 339 F.Supp. 986, 990-991 (Kan. 1972). See Truax v. Raich, 239 U.S. 33 (1915). Indeed, we do not read the appellee's brief as really asserting anything to the contrary. The "logical nexus between the status asserted and the claim sought to be adjudicated," Flast v. Cohen, 392 U.S., at 102, and the necessary degree of contentiousness, Golden v. Zwickler, 394 U.S. 103 (1969), are both present.

The appellee notes, however, that the record does not disclose that Roe was pregnant at the time of the District Court hearing on May 22, 1970, 6 or on the following June 17 when the court's opinion and judgment were filed. And he suggests that Roe's case must now be moot because she and all other members of her class are no longer subject to any 1970 pregnancy.

The usual rule in federal cases is that an actual controversy must exist at stages of appellate or certiorari review, and not simply at the date the action is initiated. United States v. Munsingwear, Inc., 340 U.S. 36 (1950); Golden v. Zwickler, supra; SEC v. Medical Committee for Human Rights, 404 U.S. 403 (1972).

But when, as here, pregnancy is a significant fact in the litigation, the normal 266-day human gestation period is so short that the pregnancy will come to term before the usual appellate process is complete. If that termination makes a case moot, pregnancy litigation seldom will survive much beyond the trial stage, and appellate review will be effectively denied. Our law should not be that rigid. Pregnancy often comes more than once to the same woman, and in the general population, if man is to survive, it will always be with us. Pregnancy provides a classic justification for a conclusion of nonmootness. It truly could be "capable of repetition, yet evading review." Southern Pacific Terminal Co. v. ICC, 219 U.S. 498, 515 (1911). See Moore v. Ogilvie, 394 U.S. 814, 816 (1969); Carroll v. Princess Anne, 393 U.S. 175, 178-179 (1968); United States v. W. T. Grant Co., 345 U.S. 629, 632-633 (1953).

We, therefore, agree with the District Court that Jane Roe had standing to undertake this litigation, that she presented a justiciable controversy, and that the termination of her 1970 pregnancy has not rendered her case moot.

B. Dr. Hallford. The doctor's position is different. He entered Roe's litigation as a plaintiff-intervenor, alleging in his complaint that he:

"In the past has been arrested for violating the Texas Abortion Laws and at the present time stands charged by indictment with violating said laws in the Criminal District Court of Dallas County, Texas to-wit: (1) The State of Texas vs. James H. Hallford, No. C-69-5307-IH, and (2) The State of Texas vs. James H. Hallford, No. C-69-2524-H. In both cases the defendant is charged with abortion . . . ."

In his application for leave to intervene, the doctor made like representations as to the abortion charges pending in the state court. These representations were also repeated in the affidavit he executed and filed in support of his motion for summary judgment.

Dr. Hallford is, therefore, in the position of seeking, in a federal court, declaratory and injunctive relief with respect to the same statutes under which he stands charged in criminal prosecutions simultaneously pending in state court. Although he stated that he has been arrested in the past for violating the State's abortion laws, he makes no allegation of any substantial and immediate threat to any federally protected right that cannot be asserted in his defense against the state prosecutions. Neither is there any allegation of harassment or bad-faith prosecution. In order to escape the rule articulated in the cases cited in the next paragraph of this opinion that, absent harassment and bad faith, a defendant in a pending state criminal case cannot affirmatively challenge in federal court the statutes under which the State is prosecuting him, Dr. Hallford seeks to distinguish his status as a present state defendant from his status as a "potential future defendant" and to assert only the latter for standing purposes here.

We see no merit in that distinction. Our decision in Samuels v. Mackell, 401 U.S. 66 (1971), compels the conclusion that the District Court erred when it granted declaratory relief to Dr. Hallford instead of refraining from so doing. The court, of course, was correct in refusing to grant injunctive relief to the doctor. The reasons supportive of that action, however, are those expressed in Samuels v. Mackell, supra, and in Younger v. Harris, 401 U.S. 37 (1971); Boyle v. Landry, 401 U.S. 77 (1971); Perez v. Ledesma, 401 U.S. 82 (1971); and Byrne v. Karalexis, 401 U.S. 216 (1971). See also Dombrowski v. Pfister, 380 U.S. 479 (1965). We note, in passing, that Younger and its companion cases were decided after the three-judge District Court decision in this case.

Dr. Hallford's complaint in intervention, therefore, is to be dismissed. [7] He is remitted to his defenses in the state criminal proceedings against him. We reverse the judgment of the District Court insofar as it granted Dr. Hallford relief and failed to dismiss his complaint in intervention.

C. The Does. In view of our ruling as to Roe's standing in her case, the issue of the Does' standing in their case has little significance. The claims they assert are essentially the same as those of Roe, and they attack the same statutes. Nevertheless, we briefly note the Does' posture.

Their pleadings present them as a childless married couple, the woman not being pregnant, who have no desire to have children at this time because of their having received medical advice that Mrs. Doe should avoid pregnancy, and for "other highly personal reasons." But they "fear . . . they may face the prospect of becoming parents." And if pregnancy ensues, they "would want to terminate" it by an abortion. They assert an inability to obtain an abortion legally in Texas and, consequently, the prospect of obtaining an illegal abortion there or of going outside Texas to some place where the procedure could be obtained legally and competently.

We thus have as plaintiffs a married couple who have, as their asserted immediate and present injury, only an alleged "detrimental effect upon [their] marital happiness" because they are forced to "the choice of refraining from normal sexual relations or of endangering Mary Doe's health through a possible pregnancy." Their claim is that sometime in the future Mrs. Doe might become pregnant because of possible failure of contraceptive measures, and at that time in the future she might want an abortion that might then be illegal under the Texas statutes.

This very phrasing of the Does' position reveals its speculative character. Their alleged injury rests on possible future contraceptive failure, possible future pregnancy, possible future unpreparedness for parenthood, and possible future impairment of health. Any one or more of these several possibilities may not take place and all may not combine. In the Does' estimation, these possibilities might have some real or imagined impact upon their marital happiness. But we are not prepared to say that the bare allegation of so indirect an injury is sufficient to present an actual case or controversy. Younger v. Harris, 401 U.S., at 41-42; Golden v. Zwickler, 394 U.S., at 109-110; Abele v. Markle, 452 F.2d, at 1124-1125; Crossen v. Breckenridge, 446 F.2d, at 839. The Does' claim falls far short of those resolved otherwise in the cases that the Does urge upon us, namely, Investment Co. Institute v. Camp, 401 U.S. 617 (1971); Data Processing Service v. Camp, 397 U.S. 150 (1970); and Epperson v. Arkansas, 393 U.S. 97 (1968). See also Truax v. Raich, 239 U.S. 33 (1915).

The Does therefore are not appropriate plaintiffs in this litigation. Their complaint was properly dismissed by the District Court, and we affirm that dismissal.

V

The principal thrust of appellant's attack on the Texas statutes is that they improperly invade a right, said to be possessed by the pregnant woman, to choose to terminate her pregnancy. Appellant would discover this right in the concept of personal "liberty" embodied in the Fourteenth Amendment's Due Process Clause; or in personal, marital, familial, and sexual privacy said to be protected by the Bill of Rights or its penumbras, see Griswold v. Connecticut, 381 U.S. 479 (1965); Eisenstadt v. Baird, 405 U.S. 438 (1972); id., at 460 (WHITE, J., concurring in result); or among those rights reserved to the people by the Ninth Amendment, Griswold v. Connecticut, 381 U.S., at 486 (Goldberg, J., concurring). Before addressing this claim, we feel it desirable briefly to survey, in several aspects, the history of abortion, for such insight as that history may afford us, and then to examine the state purposes and interests behind the criminal abortion laws.

VI

It perhaps is not generally appreciated that the restrictive criminal abortion laws in effect in a majority of States today are of relatively recent vintage. Those laws, generally proscribing abortion or its attempt at any time during pregnancy except when necessary to preserve the pregnant woman's life, are not of ancient or even of common-law origin. Instead, they derive from statutory changes effected, for the most part, in the latter half of the 19th century.

1. Ancient attitudes. These are not capable of precise determination. We are told that at the time of the Persian Empire abortifacients were known and that criminal abortions were severely punished. [8] We are also told, however, that abortion was practiced in Greek times as well as in the Roman Era, [9] and that "it was resorted to without scruple." [10] The Ephesian, Soranos, often described as the greatest of the ancient gynecologists, appears to have been generally opposed to Rome's prevailing free-abortion practices. He found it necessary to think first of the life of the mother, and he resorted to abortion when, upon this standard, he felt the procedure advisable. [11] Greek and Roman law afforded little protection to the unborn. If abortion was prosecuted in some places, it seems to have been based on a concept of a violation of the father's right to his offspring. Ancient religion did not bar abortion. [12]

2. The Hippocratic Oath. What then of the famous Oath that has stood so long as the ethical guide of the medical profession and that bears the name of the great Greek (460(?)-377(?) B. C.), who has been described as the Father of Medicine, the "wisest and the greatest practitioner of his art," and the "most important and most complete medical personality of antiquity," who dominated the medical schools of his time, and who typified the sum of the medical knowledge of the past? [13] The Oath varies somewhat according to the particular translation, but in any translation the content is clear: "I will give no deadly medicine to anyone if asked, nor suggest any such counsel; and in like manner I will not give to a woman a pessary to produce abortion," [14] or "I will neither give a deadly drug to anybody if asked for it, nor will I make a suggestion to this effect. Similarly, I will not give to a woman an abortive remedy." [15]

Although the Oath is not mentioned in any of the principal briefs in this case or in Doe v. Bolton, post, p. 179, it represents the apex of the development of strict ethical concepts in medicine, and its influence endures to this day. Why did not the authority of Hippocrates dissuade abortion practice in his time and that of Rome? The late Dr. Edelstein provides us with a theory: [16] The Oath was not uncontested even in Hippocrates' day; only the Pythagorean school of philosophers frowned upon the related act of suicide. Most Greek thinkers, on the other hand, commended abortion, at least prior to viability. See Plato, Republic, V, 461; Aristotle, Politics, VII, 1335b 25. For the Pythagoreans, however, it was a matter of dogma. For them the embryo was animate from the moment of conception, and abortion meant destruction of a living being. The abortion clause of the Oath, therefore, "echoes Pythagorean doctrines," and "in no other stratum of Greek opinion were such views held or proposed in the same spirit of uncompromising austerity." [17]

Dr. Edelstein then concludes that the Oath originated in a group representing only a small segment of Greek opinion and that it certainly was not accepted by all ancient physicians. He points out that medical writings down to Galen (A. D. 130200) "give evidence of the violation of almost every one of its injunctions." [18] But with the end of antiquity a decided change took place. Resistance against suicide and against abortion became common. The Oath came to be popular. The emerging teachings of Christianity were in agreement with the Pythagorean ethic. The Oath "became the nucleus of all medical ethics" and "was applauded as the embodiment of truth." Thus, suggests Dr. Edelstein, it is "a Pythagorean manifesto and not the expression of an absolute standard of medical conduct." [19]

This, it seems to us, is a satisfactory and acceptable explanation of the Hippocratic Oath's apparent rigidity. It enables us to understand, in historical context, a long-accepted and revered statement of medical ethics.

3. The common law. It is undisputed that at common law, abortion performed before "quickening"-- the first recognizable movement of the fetus in utero, appearing usually from the 16th to the 18th week of pregnancy[20] -- was not an indictable offense. [21] The absence of a common-law crime for pre-quickening abortion appears to have developed from a confluence of earlier philosophical, theological, and civil and canon law concepts of when life begins. These disciplines variously approached the question in terms of the point at which the embryo or fetus became "formed" or recognizably human, or in terms of when a "person" came into being, that is, infused with a "soul" or "animated." A loose consensus evolved in early English law that these events occurred at some point between conception and live birth. [22] This was "mediate animation." Although Christian theology and the canon law came to fix the point of animation at 40 days for a male and 80 days for a female, a view that persisted until the 19th century, there was otherwise little agreement about the precise time of formation or animation. There was agreement, however, that prior to this point the fetus was to be regarded as part of the mother, and its destruction, therefore, was not homicide. Due to continued uncertainty about the precise time when animation occurred, to the lack of any empirical basis for the 40-80-day view, and perhaps to Aquinas' definition of movement as one of the two first principles of life, Bracton focused upon quickening as the critical point. The significance of quickening was echoed by later common-law scholars and found its way into the received common law in this country.

Whether abortion of a quick fetus was a felony at common law, or even a lesser crime, is still disputed. Bracton, writing early in the 13th century, thought it homicide. [23] But the later and predominant view, following the great common-law scholars, has been that it was, at most, a lesser offense. In a frequently cited passage, Coke took the position that abortion of a woman "quick with child" is "a great misprision, and no murder."[24] Blackstone followed, saying that while abortion after quickening had once been considered manslaughter (though not murder), "modern law" took a less severe view.[25] A recent review of the common-law precedents argues, however, that those precedents contradict Coke and that even post-quickening abortion was never established as a common-law crime.[26] This is of some importance because while most American courts ruled, in holding or dictum, that abortion of an unquickened fetus was not criminal under their received common law,[27] others followed Coke in stating that abortion of a quick fetus was a "misprision," a term they translated to mean "misdemeanor."[28] That their reliance on Coke on this aspect of the law was uncritical and, apparently in all the reported cases, dictum (due probably to the paucity of common-law prosecutions for post-quickening abortion), makes it now appear doubtful that abortion was ever firmly established as a common-law crime even with respect to the destruction of a quick fetus.

4. The English statutory law. England's first criminal abortion statute, Lord Ellenborough's Act, 43 Geo. 3, c. 58, came in 1803. It made abortion of a quick fetus, § 1, a capital crime, but in § 2 it provided lesser penalties for the felony of abortion before quickening, and thus preserved the "quickening" distinction. This contrast was continued in the general revision of 1828, 9 Geo. 4, c. 31, § 13. It disappeared, however, together with the death penalty, in 1837, 7 Will. 4 & 1 Vict., c. 85, § 6, and did not reappear in the Offenses Against the Person Act of 1861, 24 & 25 Vict., c. 100, § 59, that formed the core of English anti-abortion law until the liberalizing reforms of 1967. In 1929, the Infant Life (Preservation) Act, 19 & 20 Geo. 5, c. 34, came into being. Its emphasis was upon the destruction of "the life of a child capable of being born alive." It made a willful act performed with the necessary intent a felony. It contained a proviso that one was not to be found guilty of the offense "unless it is proved that the act which caused the death of the child was not done in good faith for the purpose only of preserving the life of the mother."

A seemingly notable development in the English law was the case of Rex v. Bourne, [1939] 1 K. B. 687. This case apparently answered in the affirmative the question whether an abortion necessary to preserve the life of the pregnant woman was excepted from the criminal penalties of the 1861 Act. In his instructions to the jury, Judge Macnaghten referred to the 1929 Act, and observed that that Act related to "the case where a child is killed by a wilful act at the time when it is being delivered in the ordinary course of nature." Id., at 691. He concluded that the 1861 Act's use of the word "unlawfully," imported the same meaning expressed by the specific proviso in the 1929 Act, even though there was no mention of preserving the mother's life in the 1861 Act. He then construed the phrase "preserving the life of the mother" broadly, that is, "in a reasonable sense," to include a serious and permanent threat to the mother's health, and instructed the jury to acquit Dr. Bourne if it found he had acted in a good-faith belief that the abortion was necessary for this purpose. Id., at 693-694. The jury did acquit.

Recently, Parliament enacted a new abortion law. This is the Abortion Act of 1967, 15 & 16 Eliz. 2, c. 87. The Act permits a licensed physician to perform an abortion where two other licensed physicians agree (a) "that the continuance of the pregnancy would involve risk to the life of the pregnant woman, or of injury to the physical or mental health of the pregnant woman or any existing children of her family, greater than if the pregnancy were terminated," or (b) "that there is a substantial risk that if the child were born it would suffer from such physical or mental abnormalities as to be seriously handicapped." The Act also provides that, in making this determination, "account may be taken of the pregnant woman's actual or reasonably foreseeable environment." It also permits a physician, without the concurrence of others, to terminate a pregnancy where he is of the good-faith opinion that the abortion "is immediately necessary to save the life or to prevent grave permanent injury to the physical or mental health of the pregnant woman."

5. The American law. In this country, the law in effect in all but a few States until mid-19th century was the pre-existing English common law. Connecticut, the first State to enact abortion legislation, adopted in 1821 that part of Lord Ellenborough's Act that related to a woman "quick with child."[29] The death penalty was not imposed. Abortion before quickening was made a crime in that State only in 1860.[30] In 1828, New York enacted legislation[31] that, in two respects, was to serve as a model for early anti-abortion statutes. First, while barring destruction of an unquickened fetus as well as a quick fetus, it made the former only a misdemeanor, but the latter second-degree manslaughter. Second, it incorporated a concept of therapeutic abortion by providing that an abortion was excused if it "shall have been necessary to preserve the life of such mother, or shall have been advised by two physicians to be necessary for such purpose." By 1840, when Texas had received the common law,[32] only eight American States had statutes dealing with abortion.[33] It was not until after the War Between the States that legislation began generally to replace the common law. Most of these initial statutes dealt severely with abortion after quickening but were lenient with it before quickening. Most punished attempts equally with completed abortions. While many statutes included the exception for an abortion thought by one or more physicians to be necessary to save the mother's life, that provision soon disappeared and the typical law required that the procedure actually be necessary for that purpose.

Gradually, in the middle and late 19th century the quickening distinction disappeared from the statutory law of most States and the degree of the offense and the penalties were increased. By the end of the 1950's, a large majority of the jurisdictions banned abortion, however and whenever performed, unless done to save or preserve the life of the mother.34 The exceptions, Alabama and the District of Columbia, permitted abortion to preserve the mother's health.35 Three States permitted abortions that were not "unlawfully" performed or that were not "without lawful justification," leaving interpretation of those standards to the courts. 36 In the past several years, however, a trend toward liberalization of abortion statutes has resulted in adoption, by about one-third of the States, of less stringent laws, most of them patterned after the ALI Model Penal Code, § 230.3, 37 set forth as Appendix B to the opinion in Doe v. Bolton, post, p. 205.

It is thus apparent that at common law, at the time of the adoption of our Constitution, and throughout the major portion of the 19th century, abortion was viewed with less disfavor than under most American statutes currently in effect. Phrasing it another way, a woman enjoyed a substantially broader right to terminate a pregnancy than she does in most States today. At least with respect to the early stage of pregnancy, and very possibly without such a limitation, the opportunity to make this choice was present in this country well into the 19th century. Even later, the law continued for some time to treat less punitively an abortion procured in early pregnancy.

6. The position of the American Medical Association. The anti-abortion mood prevalent in this country in the late 19th century was shared by the medical profession. Indeed, the attitude of the profession may have played a significant role in the enactment of stringent criminal abortion legislation during that period.

An AMA Committee on Criminal Abortion was appointed in May 1857. It presented its report, 12 Trans. of the Am. Med. Assn. 73-78 (1859), to the Twelfth Annual Meeting. That report observed that the Committee had been appointed to investigate criminal abortion "with a view to its general suppression." It deplored abortion and its frequency and it listed three causes of "this general demoralization":

"The first of these causes is a wide-spread popular ignorance of the true character of the crime -- a belief, even among mothers themselves, that the foetus is not alive till after the period of quickening.

"The second of the agents alluded to is the fact that the profession themselves are frequently supposed careless of foetal life . . . .

"The third reason of the frightful extent of this crime is found in the grave defects of our laws, both common and statute, as regards the independent and actual existence of the child before birth, as a living being. These errors, which are sufficient in most instances to prevent conviction, are based, and only based, upon mistaken and exploded medical dogmas. With strange inconsistency, the law fully acknowledges the foetus in utero and its inherent rights, for civil purposes; while personally and as criminally affected, it fails to recognize it, and to its life as yet denies all protection." Id., at 75-76. The Committee then offered, and the Association adopted, resolutions protesting "against such unwarrantable destruction of human life," calling upon state legislatures to revise their abortion laws, and requesting the cooperation of state medical societies "in pressing the subject." Id., at 28, 78.

In 1871 a long and vivid report was submitted by the Committee on Criminal Abortion. It ended with the observation, "We had to deal with human life. In a matter of less importance we could entertain no compromise. An honest judge on the bench would call things by their proper names. We could do no less." 22 Trans. of the Am. Med. Assn. 258 (1871). It proffered resolutions, adopted by the Association, id., at 38-39, recommending, among other things, that it "be unlawful and unprofessional for any physician to induce abortion or premature labor, without the concurrent opinion of at least one respectable consulting physician, and then always with a view to the safety of the child-- if that be possible," and calling "the attention of the clergy of all denominations to the perverted views of morality entertained by a large class of females -aye, and men also, on this important question."

Except for periodic condemnation of the criminal abortionist, no further formal AMA action took place until 1967. In that year, the Committee on Human Reproduction urged the adoption of a stated policy of opposition to induced abortion, except when there is "documented medical evidence" of a threat to the health or life of the mother, or that the child "may be born with incapacitating physical deformity or mental deficiency," or that a pregnancy "resulting from legally established statutory or forcible rape or incest may constitute a threat to the mental or physical health of the patient," two other physicians "chosen because of their recognized professional competence have examined the patient and have concurred in writing, " and the procedure "is performed in a hospital accredited by the Joint Commission on Accreditation of Hospitals." The providing of medical information by physicians to state legislatures in their consideration of legislation regarding therapeutic abortion was "to be considered consistent with the principles of ethics of the American Medical Association." This recommendation was adopted by the House of Delegates. Proceedings of the AMA House of Delegates 40-51 (June 1967).

In 1970, after the introduction of a variety of proposed resolutions, and of a report from its Board of Trustees, a reference committee noted "polarization of the medical profession on this controversial issue"; division among those who had testified; a difference of opinion among AMA councils and committees; "the remarkable shift in testimony" in six months, felt to be influenced "by the rapid changes in state laws and by the judicial decisions which tend to make abortion more freely available;" and a feeling "that this trend will continue." On June 25, 1970, the House of Delegates adopted preambles and most of the resolutions proposed by the reference committee. The preambles emphasized "the best interests of the patient," "sound clinical judgment," and "informed patient consent," in contrast to "mere acquiescence to the patient's demand." The resolutions asserted that abortion is a medical procedure that should be performed by a licensed physician in an accredited hospital only after consultation with two other physicians and in conformity with state law, and that no party to the procedure should be required to violate personally held moral principles. 38 Proceedings of the AMA House of Delegates 220 (June 1970). The AMA Judicial Council rendered a complementary opinion. 39

7. The position of the American Public Health Association. In October 1970, the Executive Board of the APHA adopted Standards for Abortion Services. These were five in number:

"a. Rapid and simple abortion referral must be readily available through state and local public health departments, medical societies, or other nonprofit organizations.

"b. An important function of counseling should be to simplify and expedite the provision of abortion services; it should not delay the obtaining of these services.

"c. Psychiatric consultation should not be mandatory. As in the case of other specialized medical services, psychiatric consultation should be sought for definite indications and not on a routine basis.

"d. A wide range of individuals from appropriately trained, sympathetic volunteers to highly skilled physicians may qualify as abortion counselors.

"e. Contraception and/or sterilization should be discussed with each abortion patient." Recommended Standards for Abortion Services, 61 Am. J. Pub. Health 396 (1971).

Among factors pertinent to life and health risks associated with abortion were three that "are recognized as important":

"a. the skill of the physician,

"b. the environment in which the abortion is performed, and above all

"c. the duration of pregnancy, as determined by uterine size and confirmed by menstrual history." Id., at 397.

It was said that "a well-equipped hospital" offers more protection "to cope with unforeseen difficulties than an office or clinic without such resources. . . . The factor of gestational age is of overriding importance." Thus, it was recommended that abortions in the second trimester and early abortions in the presence of existing medical complications be performed in hospitals as inpatient procedures. For pregnancies in the first trimester, abortion in the hospital with or without overnight stay "is probably the safest practice." An abortion in an extramural facility, however, is an acceptable alternative "provided arrangements exist in advance to admit patients promptly if unforeseen complications develop." Standards for an abortion facility were listed. It was said that at present abortions should be performed by physicians or osteopaths who are licensed to practice and who have "adequate training." Id., at 398.

8. The position of the American Bar Association. At its meeting in February 1972 the ABA House of Delegates approved, with 17 opposing votes, the Uniform Abortion Act that had been drafted and approved the preceding August by the Conference of Commissioners on Uniform State Laws. 58 A. B. A. J. 380 (1972). We set forth the Act in full in the margin. [40] The Conference has appended an enlightening Prefatory Note. [41]

VII

Three reasons have been advanced to explain historically the enactment of criminal abortion laws in the 19th century and to justify their continued existence.

It has been argued occasionally that these laws were the product of a Victorian social concern to discourage illicit sexual conduct. Texas, however, does not advance this justification in the present case, and it appears that no court or commentator has taken the argument seriously. [42] The appellants and amici contend, moreover, that this is not a proper state purpose at all and suggest that, if it were, the Texas statutes are overbroad in protecting it since the law fails to distinguish between married and unwed mothers.

A second reason is concerned with abortion as a medical procedure. When most criminal abortion laws were first enacted, the procedure was a hazardous one for the woman. [43] This was particularly true prior to the development of antisepsis. Antiseptic techniques, of course, were based on discoveries by Lister, Pasteur, and others first announced in 1867, but were not generally accepted and employed until about the turn of the century. Abortion mortality was high. Even after 1900, and perhaps until as late as the development of antibiotics in the 1940's, standard modern techniques such as dilation and curettage were not nearly so safe as they are today. Thus, it has been argued that a State's real concern in enacting a criminal abortion law was to protect the pregnant woman, that is, to restrain her from submitting to a procedure that placed her life in serious jeopardy.

Modern medical techniques have altered this situation. Appellants and various amici refer to medical data indicating that abortion in early pregnancy, that is, prior to the end of the first trimester, although not without its risk, is now relatively safe. Mortality rates for women undergoing early abortions, where the procedure is legal, appear to be as low as or lower than the rates for normal childbirth. [44] Consequently, any interest of the State in protecting the woman from an inherently hazardous procedure, except when it would be equally dangerous for her to forgo it, has largely disappeared. Of course, important state interests in the areas of health and medical standards do remain. The State has a legitimate interest in seeing to it that abortion, like any other medical procedure, is performed under circumstances that insure maximum safety for the patient. This interest obviously extends at least to the performing physician and his staff, to the facilities involved, to the availability of after-care, and to adequate provision for any complication or emergency that might arise. The prevalence of high mortality rates at illegal "abortion mills" strengthens, rather than weakens, the State's interest in regulating the conditions under which abortions are performed. Moreover, the risk to the woman increases as her pregnancy continues. Thus, the State retains a definite interest in protecting the woman's own health and safety when an abortion is proposed at a late stage of pregnancy.

The third reason is the State's interest -- some phrase it in terms of duty -- in protecting prenatal life. Some of the argument for this justification rests on the theory that a new human life is present from the moment of conception. [45] The State's interest and general obligation to protect life then extends, it is argued, to prenatal life. Only when the life of the pregnant mother herself is at stake, balanced against the life she carries within her, should the interest of the embryo or fetus not prevail. Logically, of course, a legitimate state interest in this area need not stand or fall on acceptance of the belief that life begins at conception or at some other point prior to live birth. In assessing the State's interest, recognition may be given to the less rigid claim that as long as at least potential life is involved, the State may assert interests beyond the protection of the pregnant woman alone.

Parties challenging state abortion laws have sharply disputed in some courts the contention that a purpose of these laws, when enacted, was to protect prenatal life. [46] Pointing to the absence of legislative history to support the contention, they claim that most state laws were designed solely to protect the woman. Because medical advances have lessened this concern, at least with respect to abortion in early pregnancy, they argue that with respect to such abortions the laws can no longer be justified by any state interest. There is some scholarly support for this view of original purpose. [47] The few state courts called upon to interpret their laws in the late 19th and early 20th centuries did focus on the State's interest in protecting the woman's health rather than in preserving the embryo and fetus. [48] Proponents of this view point out that in many States, including Texas, [49] by statute or judicial interpretation, the pregnant woman herself could not be prosecuted for selfabortion or for cooperating in an abortion performed upon her by another. [50] They claim that adoption of the "quickening" distinction through received common law and state statutes tacitly recognizes the greater health hazards inherent in late abortion and impliedly repudiates the theory that life begins at conception.

It is with these interests, and the weight to be attached to them, that this case is concerned.

VIII

The Constitution does not explicitly mention any right of privacy. In a line of decisions, however, going back perhaps as far as Union Pacific R. Co. v. Botsford, 141 U.S. 250, 251 (1891), the Court has recognized that a right of personal privacy, or a guarantee of certain areas or zones of privacy, does exist under the Constitution. In varying contexts, the Court or individual Justices have, indeed, found at least the roots of that right in the First Amendment, Stanley v. Georgia, 394 U.S. 557, 564 (1969); in the Fourth and Fifth Amendments, Terry v. Ohio, 392 U.S. 1, 8-9 (1968), Katz v. United States, 389 U.S. 347, 350 (1967), Boyd v. United States, 116 U.S. 616 (1886), see Olmstead v. United States, 277 U.S. 438, 478 (1928) (Brandeis, J., dissenting); in the penumbras of the Bill of Rights, Griswold v. Connecticut, 381 U.S., at 484-485; in the Ninth Amendment, id., at 486 (Goldberg, J., concurring); or in the concept of liberty guaranteed by the first section of the Fourteenth Amendment, see Meyer v. Nebraska, 262 U.S. 390, 399 (1923). These decisions make it clear that only personal rights that can be deemed "fundamental" or "implicit in the concept of ordered liberty," Palko v. Connecticut, 302 U.S. 319, 325 (1937), are included in this guarantee of personal privacy. They also make it clear that the right has some extension to activities relating to marriage, Loving v. Virginia, 388 U.S. 1, 12 (1967); procreation. Skinner v. Oklahoma, 316 U.S. 535, 541-542 (1942); contraception, Eisenstadt v. Baird, 405 U.S., at 453-454; id., at 460, 463-465 (WHITE, J., concurring in result); family relationships, Prince v. Massachusetts, 321 U.S. 158, 166 (1944); and child rearing and education, Pierce v. Society of Sisters, 268 U.S. 510, 535 (1925), Meyer v. Nebraska, supra.

This right of privacy, whether it be founded in the Fourteenth Amendment's concept of personal liberty and restrictions upon state action, as we feel it is, or, as the District Court determined, in the Ninth Amendment's reservation of rights to the people, is broad enough to encompass a woman's decision whether or not to terminate her pregnancy. The detriment that the State would impose upon the pregnant woman by denying this choice altogether is apparent. Specific and direct harm medically diagnosable even in early pregnancy may be involved. Maternity. or additional offspring, may force upon the woman a distressful life and future. Psychological harm may be imminent. Mental and physical health may be taxed by child care. There is also the distress, for all concerned, associated with the unwanted child, and there is the problem of bringing a child into a family already unable, psychologically and otherwise, to care for it. In other cases, as in this one, the additional difficulties and continuing stigma of unwed motherhood may be involved. All these are factors the woman and her responsible physician necessarily will consider in consultation.

On the basis of elements such as these, appellant and some amici argue that the woman's right is absolute and that she is entitled to terminate her pregnancy at whatever time, in whatever way, and for whatever reason she alone chooses. With this we do not agree. Appellant's arguments that Texas either has no valid interest at all in regulating the abortion decision, or no interest strong enough to support any limitation upon the woman's sole determination, are unpersuasive. The Court's decisions recognizing a right of privacy also acknowledge that some state regulation in areas protected by that right is appropriate. As noted above, a State may properly assert important interests in safeguarding health, in maintaining medical standards, and in protecting potential life. At some point in pregnancy, these respective interests become sufficiently compelling to sustain regulation of the factors that govern the abortion decision. The privacy right involved, therefore, cannot be said to be absolute. In fact, it is not clear to us that the claim asserted by some amici that one has an unlimited right to do with one's body as one pleases bears a close relationship to the right of privacy previously articulated in the Court's decisions. The Court has refused to recognize an unlimited right of this kind in the past. Jacobson v. Massachusetts, 197 U.S. 11 (1905) (vaccination); Buck v. Bell, 274 U.S. 200 (1927) (sterilization).

We, therefore, conclude that the right of personal privacy includes the abortion decision, but that this right is not unqualified and must be considered against important state interests in regulation.

We note that those federal and state courts that have recently considered abortion law challenges have reached the same conclusion. A majority, in addition to the District Court in the present case, have held state laws unconstitutional, at least in part, because of vagueness or because of overbreadth and abridgment of rights. Abele v. Markle, 342 F.Supp. 800 (Conn. 1972), appeal docketed, No. 72-56; Abele v. Markle, 351 F.Supp. 224 (Conn. 1972), appeal docketed, No. 72-730; Doe v. Bolton, 319 F.Supp. 1048 (ND Ga. 1970), appeal decided today, post, p. 179; Doe v. Scott, 321 F.Supp. 1385 (ND Ill. 1971), appeal docketed, No. 70-105; Poe v. Menghini, 339 F.Supp. 986 (Kan. 1972); YWCA v. Kugler, 342 F.Supp. 1048 (NJ 1972); Babbitz v. McCann, 310 F.Supp. 293 (ED Wis. 1970), appeal dismissed, 400 U.S. 1 (1970); People v. Belous, 71 Cal. 2d 954, 458 P. 2d 194 (1969), cert. denied, 397 U.S. 915 (1970); State v. Barquet, 262 So. 2d 431 (Fla. 1972).

Others have sustained state statutes. Crossen v. Attorney General, 344 F.Supp. 587 (ED Ky. 1972), appeal docketed, No. 72-

256; Rosen v. Louisiana State Board of Medical Examiners, 318 F.Supp. 1217 (ED La. 1970), appeal docketed, No. 70-42; Corkey v. Edwards, 322 F.Supp. 1248 (WDNC 1971), appeal docketed, No. 71-92; Steinberg v. Brown, 321 F.Supp. 741 (ND Ohio 1970); Doe v. Rampton (Utah 1971), appeal docketed, No. 71-5666; Cheaney v. State, Ind. , 285 N. E. 2d 265 (1972); Spears v. State, 257 So. 2d 876 (Miss. 1972); State v. Munson, 86 S. D. 663, 201 N. W. 2d 123 (1972), appeal docketed, No. 72-631.

Although the results are divided, most of these courts have agreed that the right of privacy, however based, is broad enough to cover the abortion decision; that the right, nonetheless, is not absolute and is subject to some limitations; and that at some point the state interests as to protection of health, medical standards, and prenatal life, become dominant. We agree with this approach.

Where certain "fundamental rights" are involved, the Court has held that regulation limiting these rights may be justified only by a "compelling state interest," Kramer v. Union Free School District, 395 U.S. 621, 627 (1969); Shapiro v. Thompson, 394 U.S. 618, 634 (1969), Sherbert v. Verner, 374 U.S. 398, 406 (1963), and that legislative enactments must be narrowly drawn to express only the legitimate state interests at stake. Griswold v. Connecticut, 381 U.S., at 485; Aptheker v. Secretary of State, 378 U.S. 500, 508 (1964); Cantwell v. Connecticut, 310 U.S. 296, 307-308 (1940); see Eisenstadt v. Baird, 405 U.S., at 460, 463-464 (WHITE, J., concurring in result).

In the recent abortion cases, cited above, courts have recognized these principles. Those striking down state laws have generally scrutinized the State's interests in protecting health and potential life, and have concluded that neither interest justified broad limitations on the reasons for which a physician and his pregnant patient might decide that she should have an abortion in the early stages of pregnancy. Courts sustaining state laws have held that the State's determinations to protect health or prenatal life are dominant and constitutionally justifiable.

IX

The District Court held that the appellee failed to meet his burden of demonstrating that the Texas statute's infringement upon Roe's rights was necessary to support a compelling state interest, and that, although the appellee presented "several compelling justifications for state presence in the area of abortions," the statutes outstripped these justifications and swept "far beyond any areas of compelling state interest." 314 F.Supp., at 1222-1223. Appellant and appellee both contest that holding. Appellant, as has been indicated, claims an absolute right that bars any state imposition of criminal penalties in the area. Appellee argues that the State's determination to recognize and protect prenatal life from and after conception constitutes a compelling state interest. As noted above, we do not agree fully with either formulation.

A. The appellee and certain amici argue that the fetus is a "person" within the language and meaning of the Fourteenth Amendment. In support of this, they outline at length and in detail the wellknown facts of fetal development. If this suggestion of personhood is established, the appellant's case, of course, collapses, for the fetus' right to life would then be guaranteed specifically by the Amendment. The appellant conceded as much on reargument.[51] On the other hand, the appellee conceded on reargument [52] that no case could be cited that holds that a fetus is a person within the meaning of the Fourteenth Amendment.

The Constitution does not define "person" in so many words. Section 1 of the Fourteenth Amendment contains three references to "person." The first, in defining "citizens," speaks of "persons born or naturalized in the United States." The word also appears both in the Due Process Clause and in the Equal Protection Clause. "Person" is used in other places in the Constitution: in the listing of qualifications for Representatives and Senators, Art. I, § 2, cl. 2, and § 3, cl. 3; in the Apportionment Clause, Art. I, § 2, cl. 3; [53] in the Migration and Importation provision, Art. I, § 9, cl. 1; in the Emolument Clause, Art. I, § 9, cl. 8; in the Electors provisions, Art. II, § 1, cl. 2, and the superseded cl. 3; in the provision outlining qualifications for the office of President, Art. II, § 1, cl. 5; in the Extradition provisions, Art. IV, § 2, cl. 2, and the superseded Fugitive Slave Clause 3; and in the Fifth, Twelfth, and Twenty-second Amendments, as well as in §§ 2 and 3 of the Fourteenth Amendment. But in nearly all these instances, the use of the word is such that it has application only postnatally. None indicates, with any assurance, that it has any possible prenatal application. [54]

All this, together with our observation, supra, that throughout the major portion of the 19th century prevailing legal abortion practices were far freer than they are today, persuades us that the word "person," as used in the Fourteenth Amendment, does not include the unborn. [55] This is in accord with the results reached in those few cases where the issue has been squarely presented. McGarvey v. Magee-Womens Hospital, 340 F.Supp. 751 (WD Pa. 1972); Byrn v. New York City Health & Hospitals Corp., 31 N. Y. 2d 194, 286 N. E. 2d 887 (1972), appeal docketed, No. 72-434; Abele v. Markle, 351 F.Supp. 224 (Conn. 1972), appeal docketed, No. 72-730. Cf. Cheaney v. State, Ind., at . 285 N. E. 2d, at 270; Montana v. Rogers, 278

F.2d 68, 72 (CA7 1960), aff'd sub nom. Montana v. Kennedy, 366 U.S. 308 (1961); Keeler v. Superior Court, 2 Cal. 3d 619, 470 P. 2d 617 (1970); State v. Dickinson, 28 Ohio St. 2d 65, 275 N. E. 2d 599 (1971). Indeed, our decision in United States v. Vuitch, 402 U.S. 62 (1971), inferentially is to the same effect, for we there would not have indulged in statutory interpretation favorable to abortion in specified circumstances if the necessary consequence was the termination of life entitled to Fourteenth Amendment protection.

This conclusion, however, does not of itself fully answer the contentions raised by Texas, and we pass on to other considerations.

B. The pregnant woman cannot be isolated in her privacy. She carries an embryo and, later, a fetus, if one accepts the medical definitions of the developing young in the human uterus. See Dorland's Illustrated Medical Dictionary 478479, 547 (24th ed. 1965). The situation therefore is inherently different from marital intimacy, or bedroom possession of obscene material, or marriage, or procreation, or education, with which Eisenstadt and Griswold, Stanley, Loving, Skinner, and Pierce and Meyer were respectively concerned. As we have intimated above, it is reasonable and appropriate for a State to decide that at some point in time another interest, that of health of the mother or that of potential human life, becomes significantly involved. The woman's privacy is no longer sole and any right of privacy she possesses must be measured accordingly.

Texas urges that, apart from the Fourteenth Amendment, life begins at conception and is present throughout pregnancy, and that, therefore, the State has a compelling interest in protecting that life from and after conception. We need not resolve the difficult question of when life begins. When those trained in the respective disciplines of medicine, philosophy, and theology are unable to arrive at any consensus, the judiciary, at this point in the development of man's knowledge, is not in a position to speculate as to the answer.

It should be sufficient to note briefly the wide divergence of thinking on this most sensitive and difficult question. There has always been strong support for the view that life does not begin until live birth. This was the belief of the Stoics. [56]It appears to be the predominant, though not the unanimous, attitude of the Jewish faith. [57]It may be taken to represent also the position of a large segment of the Protestant community, insofar as that can be ascertained; organized groups that have taken a formal position on the abortion issue have generally regarded abortion as a matter for the conscience of the individual and her family. [58] As we have noted, the common law found greater significance in quickening. Physicians and their scientific colleagues have regarded that event with less interest and have tended to focus either upon conception, upon live birth, or upon the interim point at which the fetus becomes "viable," that is, potentially able to live outside the mother's womb, albeit with artificial aid. [59] Viability is usually placed at about seven months (28 weeks) but may occur earlier, even at 24 weeks. [60] The Aristotelian theory of "mediate animation," that held sway throughout the Middle Ages and the Renaissance in Europe, continued to be official Roman Catholic dogma until the 19th century, despite opposition to this "ensoulment" theory from those in the Church who would recognize the existence of life from the moment of conception. [61] The latter is now, of course, the official belief of the Catholic Church. As one brief amicus discloses, this is a view strongly held by many non-Catholics as well, and by many physicians. Substantial problems for precise definition of this view are posed, however, by new embryological data that purport to indicate that conception is a "process" over time. rather than an event, and by new medical techniques such as menstrual extraction, the "morning after" pill, implantation of embryos, artificial insemination, and even artificial wombs. [62]

In areas other than criminal abortion, the law has been reluctant to endorse any theory that life, as we recognize it, begins before live birth or to accord legal rights to the unborn except in narrowly defined situations and except when the rights are contingent upon live birth. For example, the traditional rule of tort law denied recovery for prenatal injuries even though the child was born alive. [63] That rule has been changed in almost every jurisdiction. In most States, recovery is said to be permitted only if the fetus was viable, or at least quick, when the injuries were sustained, though few courts have squarely so held. [64] In a recent development, generally opposed by the commentators, some States permit the parents of a stillborn child to maintain an action for wrongful death because of prenatal injuries. [65]Such an action, however, would appear to be one to vindicate the parents' interest and is thus consistent with the view that the fetus, at most, represents only the potentiality of life. Similarly, unborn children have been recognized as acquiring rights or interests by way of inheritance or other devolution of property, and have been represented by guardians ad litem. [66]Perfection of the interests involved, again, has generally been contingent upon live birth. In short, the unborn have never been recognized in the law as persons in the whole sense.

X

In view of all this, we do not agree that, by adopting one theory of life, Texas may override the rights of the pregnant woman that are at stake. We repeat, however, that the State does have an important and legitimate interest in preserving and protecting the health of the pregnant woman, whether she be a resident of the State or a nonresident who seeks medical consultation and treatment there, and that it has still another important and legitimate interest in protecting the potentiality of human life. These interests are separate and distinct. Each grows in substantiality as the woman approaches term and, at a point during pregnancy, each becomes "compelling."

With respect to the State's important and legitimate interest in the health of the mother, the "compelling" point, in the light of present medical knowledge, is at approximately the end of the first trimester. This is so because of the now established medical fact, referred to above at 149, that until the end of the first trimester mortality in abortion may be less than mortality in normal childbirth. It follows that, from and after this point, a State may regulate the abortion procedure to the extent that the regulation reasonably relates to the preservation and protection of maternal health. Examples of permissible state regulation in this area are requirements as to the qualifications of the person who is to perform the abortion; as to the licensure of that person; as to the facility in which the procedure is to be performed, that is, whether it must be a hospital or may be a clinic or some other place of less-than-hospital status; as to the licensing of the facility; and the like.

This means, on the other hand, that, for the period of pregnancy prior to this "compelling" point, the attending physician, in consultation with his patient, is free to determine, without regulation by the State, that, in his medical judgment, the patient's pregnancy should be terminated. If that decision is reached, the judgment may be effectuated by an abortion free of interference by the State.

With respect to the State's important and legitimate interest in potential life, the "compelling" point is at viability. This is so because the fetus then presumably has the capability of meaningful life outside the mother's womb. State regulation protective of fetal life after viability thus has both logical and biological justifications. If the State is interested in protecting fetal life after viability, it may go so far as to proscribe abortion during that period, except when it is necessary to preserve the life or health of the mother.

Measured against these standards, Art. 1196 of the Texas Penal Code, in restricting legal abortions to those "procured or attempted by medical advice for the purpose of saving the life of the mother," sweeps too broadly. The statute makes no distinction between abortions performed early in pregnancy and those performed later, and it limits to a single reason, "saving" the mother's life, the legal justification for the procedure. The statute, therefore, cannot survive the constitutional attack made upon it here.

This conclusion makes it unnecessary for us to consider the additional challenge to the Texas statute asserted on grounds of vagueness. See United States v. Vuitch, 402 U.S., at 67-72.

XI

To summarize and to repeat:

1. A state criminal abortion statute of the current Texas type, that excepts from criminality only a lifesaving procedure on behalf of the mother, without regard to pregnancy stage and without recognition of the other interests involved, is violative of the Due Process Clause of the Fourteenth Amendment.

(a) For the stage prior to approximately the end of the first trimester, the abortion decision and its effectuation must be left to the medical judgment of the pregnant woman's attending physician.

(b) For the stage subsequent to approximately the end of the first trimester, the State, in promoting its interest in the health of the mother, may, if it chooses, regulate the abortion procedure in ways that are reasonably related to maternal health.

(c) For the stage subsequent to viability, the State in promoting its interest in the potentiality of human life may, if it chooses, regulate, and even proscribe, abortion except where it is necessary, in appropriate medical judgment, for the preservation of the life or health of the mother.

2. The State may define the term "physician," as it has been employed in the preceding paragraphs of this Part XI of this opinion, to mean only a physician currently licensed by the State, and may proscribe any abortion by a person who is not a physician as so defined.

In Doe v. Bolton, post, p. 179, procedural requirements contained in one of the modern abortion statutes are considered. That opinion and this one, of course, are to be read together. 67

This holding, we feel, is consistent with the relative weights of the respective interests involved, with the lessons and examples of medical and legal history, with the lenity of the common law, and with the demands of the profound problems of the present day. The decision leaves the State free to place increasing restrictions on abortion as the period of pregnancy lengthens, so long as those restrictions are tailored to the recognized state interests. The decision vindicates the right of the physician to administer medical treatment according to his professional judgment up to the points where important state interests provide compelling justifications for intervention. Up to those points, the abortion decision in all its aspects is inherently, and primarily, a medical decision, and basic responsibility for it must rest with the physician. If an individual practitioner abuses the privilege of exercising proper medical judgment, the usual remedies, judicial and intraprofessional, are available.

XII

Our conclusion that Art. 1196 is unconstitutional means, of course, that the Texas abortion statutes, as a unit, must fall. The exception of Art. 1196 cannot be struck down separately, for then the State would be left with a statute proscribing all abortion procedures no matter how medically urgent the case.

Although the District Court granted appellant Roe declaratory relief, it stopped short of issuing an injunction against enforcement of the Texas statutes. The Court has recognized that different considerations enter into a federal court's decision as to declaratory relief, on the one hand, and injunctive relief, on the other. Zwickler v. Koota, 389 U.S. 241. 252255 (1967); Dombrowski v. Pfister, 380 U.S. 479 (1965). We are not dealing with a statute that, on its face, appears to abridge free expression, an area of particular concern under Dombrowski and refined in Younger v. Harris. 401 U.S., at 50.

We find it unnecessary to decide whether the District Court erred in withholding injunctive relief, for we assume the Texas prosecutorial authorities will give full credence to this decision that the present criminal abortion statutes of that State are unconstitutional.

The judgment of the District Court as to intervenor Hallford is reversed, and Dr. Hallford's complaint in intervention is dismissed. In all other respects, the judgment of the District Court is affirmed. Costs are allowed to the appellee.

It is so ordered.

---- Begin EndNotes ----

: "Article 1191. Abortion

"If any person shall designedly administer to a pregnant woman or knowingly procure to be administered with her consent any drug or medicine, or shall use towards her any violence or means whatever externally or internally applied, and thereby procure an abortion, he shall be confined in the penitentiary not less than two nor more than five years; if it be done without her consent, the punishment shall be doubled. By 'abortion' is meant that the life of the fetus or embryo shall be destroyed in the woman's womb or that a premature birth thereof be caused.

"Art. 1192. Furnishing the means

"Whoever furnishes the means for procuring an abortion knowing the purpose intended is guilty as an accomplice.

"Art. 1193. Attempt at abortion

"If the means used shall fail to produce an abortion, the offender is nevertheless guilty of an attempt to produce abortion, provided it be shown that such means were calculated to produce that result, and shall be fined not less than one hundred nor more than one thousand dollars.

"Art. 1194. Murder in producing abortion

"If the death of the mother is occasioned by an abortion so produced or by an attempt to effect the same it is murder."

"Art. 1196. By medical advice

"Nothing in this chapter applies to an abortion procured or attempted by medical advice for the purpose of saving the life of the mother."

The foregoing Articles, together with Art. 1195, compose Chapter 9 of Title 15 of the Penal Code. Article 1195, not attacked here, reads:

"Art. 1195. Destroying unborn child

"Whoever shall during parturition of the mother destroy the vitality or life in a child in a state of being born and before actual birth, which child would otherwise have been born alive, shall be confined in the penitentiary for life or for not less than five years."

2 Ariz. Rev. Stat. Ann. § 13-211 (1956); Conn. Pub. Act No. 1 (May 1972 special session) (in 4 Conn. Leg. Serv. 677 (1972)), and Conn. Gen. Stat. Rev. §§ 53-29, 53-30 (1968) (or unborn child); Idaho Code § 18-601 (1948); Ill. Rev. Stat., c. 38, § 23-1 (1971); Ind. Code § 35-1-58-1 (1971); Iowa Code § 701.1 (1971); Ky. Rev. Stat. § 436.020 (1962); La. Rev. Stat. § 37:1285 (6) (1964) (loss of medical license) (but see § 14:87 (Supp. 1972) containing no exception for the life of the mother under the criminal statute); Me. Rev. Stat. Ann., Tit. 17, § 51 (1964); Mass. Gen. Laws Ann., c. 272, § 19 (1970) (using the term "unlawfully," construed to exclude an abortion to save the mother's life, Kudish v. Bd. of Registration, 356 Mass. 98, 248 N. E. 2d 264 (1969)); Mich. Comp. Laws § 750.14 (1948); Minn. Stat. § 617.18 (1971); Mo. Rev. Stat. § 559.100 (1969); Mont. Rev. Codes Ann. § 94-401 (1969); Neb. Rev. Stat. § 28-405 (1964); Nev. Rev. Stat. § 200.220 (1967); N. H. Rev. Stat. Ann. § 585:13 (1955); N. J. Stat. Ann. § 2A:87-1 (1969) ("without lawful justification"); N. D. Cent. Code §§ 12-25-01, 12-25-02 (1960); Ohio Rev. Code Ann. § 2901.16 (1953); Okla. Stat. Ann., Tit. 21, § 861 (1972-1973 Supp.); Pa. Stat. Ann., Tit. 18, §§ 4718, 4719 (1963) ("unlawful"); R. I. Gen. Laws Ann. § 11-3-1 (1969); S. D. Comp. Laws Ann. § 22-17-1 (1967); Tenn. Code Ann. §§ 39-301, 39-302 (1956); Utah Code Ann. §§ 76-2-1, 76-2-2 (1953); Vt. Stat. Ann., Tit. 13, § 101 (1958); W. Va. Code Ann. § 61-2-8 (1966); Wis. Stat. § 940.04 (1969); Wyo. Stat. Ann. §§ 6-77, 6-78 (1957).

3 Long ago, a suggestion was made that the Texas statutes were unconstitutionally vague because of definitional deficiencies. The Texas Court of Criminal Appeals disposed of that suggestion peremptorily, saying only,

"It is also insisted in the motion in arrest of judgment that the statute is unconstitutional and void in that it does not sufficiently define or describe the offense of abortion. We do not concur in respect to this question." Jackson v. State, 55 Tex. Cr. R. 79, 89, 115 S. W. 262, 268 (1908).

The same court recently has held again that the State's abortion statutes are not unconstitutionally vague or overbroad. Thompson v. State (Ct. Crim. App. Tex. 1971), appeal docketed, No. 71-1200. The court held that "the State of Texas has a compelling interest to protect fetal life"; that Art. 1191 "is designed to protect fetal life"; that the Texas homicide statutes, particularly Art. 1205 of the Penal Code, are intended to protect a person "in existence by actual birth" and thereby implicitly recognize other human life that is not "in existence by actual birth"; that the definition of human life is for the legislature and not the courts; that Art. 1196 "is more definite than the District of Columbia statute upheld in [United States v.] Vuitch" (402 U.S. 62); and that the Texas statute "is not vague and indefinite or overbroad." A physician's abortion conviction was affirmed.

In Thompson, n. 2, the court observed that any issue as to the burden of proof under the exemption of Art. 1196 "is not before us." But see Veevers v. State, 172 Tex. Cr. R. 162, 168-169, 354 S. W. 2d 161, 166-167 (1962). Cf. United States v. Vuitch, 402 U.S. 62, 69-71 (1971).

4 The name is a pseudonym.

5 These names are pseudonyms.

6 The appellee twice states in his brief that the hearing before the District Court was held on July 22, 1970. Brief for Appellee 13. The docket entries, App. 2, and the transcript, App. 76, reveal this to be an error. The July date appears to be the time of the reporter's transcription. See App. 77.

7 We need not consider what different result, if any, would follow if Dr. Hallford's intervention were on behalf of a class. His complaint in intervention does not purport to assert a class suit and makes no reference to any class apart from an allegation

CHAPTER THREE   THE ACT

Next I moved into getting a copy of the Unborn Victims of Violence Act. Interesting to read, here is a copy.

H. R. 1997

One Hundred Eighth Congress
of the
United States of America

AT THE SECOND SESSION

Begun and held at the City of Washington on Tuesday,
the twentieth day of January, two thousand and four

An Act

To amend title 18, United States Code, and the Uniform Code of Military Justice
to protect unborn children from assault and murder, and for other purposes.

Be it enacted by the Senate and House of Representatives of
the United States of America in Congress assembled,

SECTION 1. SHORT TITLE.

This Act may be cited as the "Unborn Victims of Violence Act of 2004" or "Laci and Conner's Law".

SEC. 2. PROTECTION OF UNBORN CHILDREN.

(a) IN GENERAL.—Title 18, United States Code, is amended by inserting after chapter 90 the following:

"CHAPTER 90A—PROTECTION OF UNBORN CHILDREN

"Sec.
"1841. Protection of unborn children.

"§ 1841. Protection of unborn children

"(a)(1) Whoever engages in conduct that violates any of the provisions of law listed in subsection (b) and thereby causes the death of, or bodily injury (as defined in section 1365) to, a child, who is in utero at the time the conduct takes place, is guilty of a separate offense under this section.

"(2)(A) Except as otherwise provided in this paragraph, the punishment for that separate offense is the same as the punishment provided under Federal law for that conduct had that injury or death occurred to the unborn child's mother.

"(B) An offense under this section does not require proof that—

"(i) the person engaging in the conduct had knowledge or should have had knowledge that the victim of the underlying offense was pregnant; or

"(ii) the defendant intended to cause the death of, or bodily injury to, the unborn child.

"(C) If the person engaging in the conduct thereby intentionally kills or attempts to kill the unborn child, that person shall instead of being punished under subparagraph (A), be punished as provided under sections 1111, 1112, and 1113 of this title for intentionally killing or attempting to kill a human being.

"(D) Notwithstanding any other provision of law, the death penalty shall not be imposed for an offense under this section.

"(b) The provisions referred to in subsection (a) are the following:

"(1) Sections 36, 37, 43, 111, 112, 113, 114, 115, 229, 242, 245, 247, 248, 351, 831, 844(d), (f), (h)(1), and (i), 924(j),

930, 1111, 1112, 1113, 1114, 1116, 1118, 1119, 1120, 1121, 1153(a), 1201(a), 1203, 1365(a), 1501, 1503, 1505, 1512, 1513, 1751, 1864, 1951, 1952 (a)(1)(B), (a)(2)(B), and (a)(3)(B), 1958, 1959, 1992, 2113, 2114, 2116, 2118, 2119, 2191, 2231, 2241(a), 2245, 2261, 2261A, 2280, 2281, 2332, 2332a, 2332b, 2340A, and 2441 of this title.

"(2) Section 408(e) of the Controlled Substances Act of 1970 (21 U.S.C. 848(e)).

"(3) Section 202 of the Atomic Energy Act of 1954 (42 U.S.C. 2283).

"(c) Nothing in this section shall be construed to permit the prosecution—

"(1) of any person for conduct relating to an abortion for which the consent of the pregnant woman, or a person authorized by law to act on her behalf, has been obtained or for which such consent is implied by law;

"(2) of any person for any medical treatment of the pregnant woman or her unborn child; or

"(3) of any woman with respect to her unborn child.

"(d) As used in this section, the term 'unborn child' means a child in utero, and the term 'child in utero' or 'child, who is in utero' means a member of the species homo sapiens, at any stage of development, who is carried in the womb.".

(b) CLERICAL AMENDMENT.—The table of chapters for part I of title 18, United States Code, is amended by inserting after the item relating to chapter 90 the following new item:

"90A. Protection of unborn children .... 1841".

SEC. 3. MILITARY JUSTICE SYSTEM.

(a) PROTECTION OF UNBORN CHILDREN.—Subchapter X of chapter 47 of title 10, United States Code (the Uniform Code of Military Justice), is amended by inserting after section 919 (article 119) the following new section:

"§ 919a. Art. 119a. Death or injury of an unborn child

"(a)(1) Any person subject to this chapter who engages in conduct that violates any of the provisions of law listed in subsection (b) and thereby causes the death of, or bodily injury (as defined in section 1365 of title 18) to, a child, who is in utero at the time the conduct takes place, is guilty of a separate offense under this section and shall, upon conviction, be punished by such punishment, other than death, as a court-martial may direct, which shall be consistent with the punishments prescribed by the President for that conduct had that injury or death occurred to the unborn child's mother.

"(2) An offense under this section does not require proof that—

"(i) the person engaging in the conduct had knowledge or should have had knowledge that the victim of the underlying offense was pregnant; or

"(ii) the accused intended to cause the death of, or bodily injury to, the unborn child.

"(3) If the person engaging in the conduct thereby intentionally kills or attempts to kill the unborn child, that person shall, instead of being punished under paragraph (1), be punished as provided under sections 880, 918, and 919(a) of this title (articles 80, 118, and 119(a)) for intentionally killing or attempting to kill a human being.

H. R. 1997—3

"(4) Notwithstanding any other provision of law, the death penalty shall not be imposed for an offense under this section.

"(b) The provisions referred to in subsection (a) are sections 918, 919(a), 919(b)(2), 920(a), 922, 924, 926, and 928 of this title (articles 118, 119(a), 119(b)(2), 120(a), 122, 124, 126, and 128).

"(c) Nothing in this section shall be construed to permit the prosecution—

"(1) of any person for conduct relating to an abortion for which the consent of the pregnant woman, or a person authorized by law to act on her behalf, has been obtained or for which such consent is implied by law;

"(2) of any person for any medical treatment of the pregnant woman or her unborn child; or

"(3) of any woman with respect to her unborn child.

"(d) In this section, the term 'unborn child' means a child in utero, and the term 'child in utero' or 'child, who is in utero' means a member of the species homo sapiens, at any stage of development, who is carried in the womb.".

(b) CLERICAL AMENDMENT.—The table of sections at the beginning of such subchapter is amended by inserting after the item relating to section 919 the following new item:

"919a. 119a. Death or injury of an unborn child.".

Speaker of the House of Representatives.

Vice President of the United States and
President of the Senate.

CHAPTER FOUR   THE RESEARCH

I started as basic as I could, with the beginning of the Constitution of the United States of America. Not hard to read and letting me know that the "blessing of liberty to ourselves and our posterity" were "secure" with this Constitution.

If all went well, I needed to find out where to serve the suit. I found that on the United States Department of Justice website.

Finally, I pulled up every protection the Unborn Victim of Violence Act provides the human being in utero. Again, interesting reading.

My basis of the Complaint was that the Unborn Victims of Violence Act named every conceivable way the human being in utero was protected against death (with abortion being the only cause permissible) from the moment of conception. The most important thing I found in the Act was that it noted that life began at the moment of conception. It hit me that this was what the pro-life organizations needed to repeal Roe v. Wade.

So, logically, if life begins at the moment of conception, and the human being was conceived in the United States of America, then that person has the same unalienable rights as a human being out of utero. Simple stuff.

But still, no one was doing a thing, still no suits filed. I kept digging. I pulled all the various ways of protection the Act afforded the human being in utero and they became part of my research and ultimately part of the Complaint.

One of the protections was death by manslaughter. Now, there are different degrees of manslaughter. The manslaughter definition I focused on was, as described by Title 18, ". . . a legal act that results in death."

The Act references ". . . at any stage of development…" and even goes so far as to refer to this human being as ". . . homo sapiens. . ." and ". . . child(ren)…".

So, if life begins for a child(ren) at the moment of conception (at any stage of development), and protections are afforded against various types of crimes committed against the mother that would then affect the human being in utero, it only makes sense that manslaughter (a legal act that results in death) perpetrated upon the mother and then ultimately affecting the human being in utero would apply to both. An example, a driver of a vehicle not paying attention and kills someone, you get the drift.

Well, if manslaughter is a legal act that results in death, and life is recognized for the human being in utero from the moment of conception, then quite simply, abortion would be a legal act that results in death.

With my research done, I now had to build a case.

legal information institute   **U.S. Constitution**

collection home   search

The Constitution of the United States of America

We the people of the United States, in order to form a more perfect union, establish justice, insure domestic tranquility, provide for the common defense, promote the general welfare, and secure the blessings of liberty to ourselves and our posterity, do ordain and establish this Constitution for the United States of America.

- Table of Articles and Amendments
- Overview of Full Constitution

copyright   about us   send email

HOMEPAGE | CONTACT US | PRIVACY POLICY | SITE MAP | SEARCH

About DOJ
Publications & Documents
Press Room
Employment
Doing Business with DOJ
FOIA
Grants
Fugitives & Missing Persons

Other Federal Sites

Last Updated: 3/29/04

Contact Us

BY MAIL:

Correspondence to the Department, including the Attorney General, may be sent to:

U.S. Department of Justice
950 Pennsylvania Avenue, NW
Washington, DC 20530-0001

BY E-MAIL:

E-mails to the Department of Justice, including the Attorney General, may be sent to AskDOJ@usdoj.gov.

E-mails will be forwarded to the responsible Department of Justice component for appropriate handling. Before sending e-mail, please read our Privacy Policy for details about how we handle personal information.

If you know the specific organization or official you wish to contact, please indicate such in your message or check the Component Contact Information Page to contact them directly.

Please include your mailing address in the event that the Department replies via United States Postal Service.

To Comment on the USDOJ Website, please email webmaster@usdoj.gov.

BY PHONE:

Office of the Attorney General - 202-353-1555

To call component officials, see the Directory of Department Officials

To call an individual employee, search the DOJ Employee Directory

OTHER CONTACT INFORMATION:

Component Contact Information Page

FOIA Contacts

To Report Unsolicited Commercial E-Mail ("Spam")

To Report Child Pornography and/or Sexual Exploitation of Children
Contact the Crimes Against Children Coordinator at your local FBI Field

Office or the National Center for Missing and Exploited Children's CyberTipline.

To Report a Complaint about Violation of your Civil Rights or Civil Liberties by a Department of Justice Employee

To Report a Complaint about Waste, Fraud, Abuse, or Misconduct in the Department of Justice

RESPONSES TO E-MAIL:

Thank you for visiting the Department's "Contact Us" page. On behalf of the Attorney General, the Department of Justice would like to thank you for your many e-mail messages on law enforcement issues and activities and other matters of special interest to many groups across the nation. The Attorney General appreciates the fact that so many citizens have taken the time to express their views and thoughts on these important matters. In some instances, however, the volume of e-mail traffic on a particular issue is such that we cannot respond to each message individually. We would like you to know, however, that all incoming messages are forwarded to the appropriate organization within the Department of Justice and you can be assured that your voices and views are being heard.

LII
legal information institute

collection home

US CODE COLLECTION

search

Search this title:

Search Title 18

Notes
Updates
Parallel authorities
(CFR)
Topical references

Sec. 36. - Drive-by shooting

(a) Definition. -

In this section, "major drug offense" means -

(1)

a continuing criminal enterprise punishable under section 408(c) of the Controlled Substances Act (21 U.S.C. 848(c));

(2)

a conspiracy to distribute controlled substances punishable under section 406 of the Controlled Substances Act (21 U.S.C. 846) section [1] 1013 of the Controlled Substances Import and Export Act (21 U.S.C. 963); or "or".

(3)

an offense involving major quantities of drugs and punishable under section 401(b)(1)(A) of the Controlled Substances Act (21 U.S.C. 841(b)(1)(A)) or section 1010 (b)(1) of the Controlled Substances Import and Export Act (21 U.S.C. 960(b)(1)).

(b) Offense and Penalties. -

(1)

A person who, in furtherance or to escape detection of a major drug offense and with the intent to intimidate, harass, injure, or maim, fires a weapon into a group of two or more persons and who, in the course of such conduct, causes grave risk to any human life shall be punished by a term of no more than 25 years, by fine under this title, or both.

(2)

A person who, in furtherance or to escape detection of a major drug offense and with the intent to intimidate, harass, injure, or maim, fires a weapon into a group of 2 or more persons and who, in the course of such conduct, kills any person shall, if the killing -

(A)

is a first degree murder (as defined in section 1111(a)), be punished by death or imprisonment for any term of years or for life, fined under this title, or both; or

(B)

is a murder other than a first degree murder (as defined in section 1111(a)), be fined under this title, imprisoned for any term of years or for life, or both

---

[1] So in original. Probably should be preceded by

Prev | Next

US CODE COLLECTION

search

TITLE 18 > **PART I** > **CHAPTER 2** > **Sec. 37.**   Prev | Next

Search this title:

Search Title 18

Notes
Updates
Parallel authorities
(CFR)
Topical references

Sec. 37. - Violence at international airports

(a) Offense. -

A person who unlawfully and intentionally, using any device, substance, or weapon -

(1)

performs an act of violence against a person at an airport serving international civil aviation that causes or is likely to cause serious bodily injury (as defined in section 1365 of this title) or death; or

(2)

destroys or seriously damages the facilities of an airport serving international civil aviation or a civil aircraft not in service located thereon or disrupts the services of the airport,

if such an act endangers or is likely to endanger safety at that airport, or attempts or conspires to do such an act, shall be fined under this title, imprisoned not more than 20 years, or both; and if the death of any person results from conduct prohibited by this subsection, shall be punished by death or imprisoned for any term of years or for life.

(b) Jurisdiction. -

There is jurisdiction over the prohibited activity in subsection (a) if -

(1)

the prohibited activity takes place in the United States; or

(2)

the prohibited activity takes place outside the United

States and

(A)

the offender is later found in the United States; or

(B)

an offender or a victim is a national of the United States (as defined in section 101(a)(22) of the Immigration and Nationality Act (8 U.S.C. 1101(a)(22))).

(c) Bar to Prosecution. -

It is a bar to Federal prosecution under subsection (a) for conduct that occurred within the United States that the conduct involved was during or in relation to a labor dispute, and such conduct is prohibited as a felony under the law of the State in which it was committed. For purposes of this section, the term "labor dispute" has the meaning set forth in section 2(c) [1] of the Norris-LaGuardia Act, as amended (29 U.S.C. 113(c)), and the term "State" means a State of the United States, the District of Columbia, and any commonwealth, territory, or possession of the United States. "13(c)".

---

[1] So in original. Probably should be section

Prev | Next

legal information institute

collection home

US CODE COLLECTION

search

TITLE 18 > PART I > CHAPTER 3 > Sec. 43.

Prev | Next

Sec. 43. - Animal enterprise terrorism

(a) Offense. -

Whoever -

(1)

travels in interstate or foreign commerce, or uses or causes to be used the mail or any facility in interstate or foreign commerce, for the purpose of causing physical disruption to the functioning of an animal enterprise; and

(2)

intentionally causes physical disruption to the functioning of an animal enterprise by intentionally stealing, damaging, or causing the loss of, any property (including animals or records) used by the animal enterprise, and thereby causes economic damage exceeding $10,000 to that enterprise, or conspires to do so;

shall be fined under this title or imprisoned not more than one year, or both.

(b) Aggravated Offense. -

(1) Serious bodily injury. -

Whoever in the course of a violation of subsection (a) causes serious bodily injury to another individual shall be fined under this title or imprisoned not more than 10 years, or both.

(2) Death. -

Whoever in the course of a violation of subsection (a) causes the death of an individual shall be fined under this title and imprisoned for life or for any term of years.

Search this title:

Search Title 18

Notes
Updates
Parallel authorities
(CFR)
Topical references

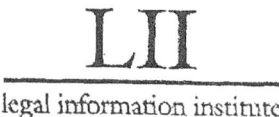

US CODE COLLECTION

search

<u>TITLE 18</u> > PART I > CHAPTER 7 > Sec. 111.   Next

Sec. 111. - Assaulting, resisting, or impeding certain officers or employees

(a) In General. -

Whoever -

(1)

forcibly assaults, resists, opposes, impedes, intimidates, or interferes with any person designated in section 1114 of this title while engaged in or on account of the performance of official duties; or

(2)

forcibly assaults or intimidates any person who formerly served as a person designated in section 1114 on account of the performance of official duties during such person's term of service,

shall, where the acts in violation of this section constitute only simple assault, be fined under this title or imprisoned not more than one year, or both, and in all other cases, be fined under this title or imprisoned not more than three years, or both.

(b) Enhanced Penalty. -

Whoever, in the commission of any acts described in subsection (a), uses a deadly or dangerous weapon (including a weapon intended to cause death or danger but that fails to do so by reason of a defective component) or inflicts bodily injury, shall be fined under this title or imprisoned not more than ten years, or both.

Search this title:

Search Title 18

Notes
Updates
Parallel authorities (CFR)
Topical references

Next

(c) Restitution. -

An order of restitution under section 3663 or 3663A of this title with respect to a violation of this section may also include restitution -

(1)

for the reasonable cost of repeating any experimentation that was interrupted or invalidated as a result of the offense; and

(2)

the loss of food production or farm income reasonably attributable to the offense.

(d) Definitions. -

As used in this section -

(1)

the term "animal enterprise" means -

(A)

a commercial or academic enterprise that uses animals for food or fiber production, agriculture, research, or testing;

(B)

a zoo, aquarium, circus, rodeo, or lawful competitive animal event; or

(C)

any fair or similar event intended to advance agricultural arts and sciences;

(2)

the term "physical disruption" does not include any lawful disruption that results from lawful public, governmental, or animal enterprise employee reaction to the disclosure of information about an animal enterprise;

(3)

the term "economic damage" means the replacement costs of lost or damaged property or records, the costs of repeating an interrupted or invalidated experiment, or the loss of profits; and

(4)

the term "serious bodily injury" has the meaning given that term in section 1365 of this title.

(e) Non-Preemption. -

Nothing in this section preempts any State law.

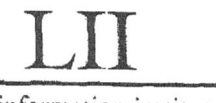

US CODE COLLECTION

TITLE 18 > PART I > CHAPTER 7 > Sec. 112.　　　Prev | Next

Search this title:

[Search Title 18]

Notes
Updates
Parallel authorities
(CFR)
Topical references

Sec. 112. - Protection of foreign officials, official guests, and internationally protected persons

(a)

Whoever assaults, strikes, wounds, imprisons, or offers violence to a foreign official, official guest, or internationally protected person or makes any other violent attack upon the person or liberty of such person, or, if likely to endanger his person or liberty, makes a violent attack upon his official premises, private accommodation, or means of transport or attempts to commit any of the foregoing shall be fined under this title or imprisoned not more than three years, or both. Whoever in the commission of any such act uses a deadly or dangerous weapon, or inflicts bodily injury, shall be fined under this title or imprisoned not more than ten years, or both.

(b)

Whoever willfully -

(1)

intimidates, coerces, threatens, or harasses a foreign official or an official guest or obstructs a foreign official in the performance of his duties;

(2)

attempts to intimidate, coerce, threaten, or harass a foreign official or an official guest or obstruct a foreign official in the performance of his duties; or

(3)

within the United States and within one hundred feet of any building or premises in whole or in part owned, used, or occupied for official business or for diplomatic, consular, or residential purposes by -

(A)

a foreign government, including such use as a mission to an international organization;

(B)

an international organization;

(C)

a foreign official; or

(D)

an official guest;

congregates with two or more other persons with intent to violate any other provision of this section; shall be fined under this title or imprisoned not more than six months, or both.

(c)

For the purpose of this section "foreign government", "foreign official", "internationally protected person", "international organization", "national of the United States", and "official guest" shall have the same meanings as those provided in section 1116(b) of this title.

(d)

Nothing contained in this section shall be construed or applied so as to abridge the exercise of rights guaranteed under the first amendment to the Constitution of the United States.

(e)

If the victim of an offense under subsection (a) is an internationally protected person outside the United States, the United States may exercise jurisdiction over the offense if

(1)

the victim is a representative, officer, employee, or agent of the United States,

(2)

an offender is a national of the United States, or

(3)

an offender is afterwards found in the United States.

As used in this subsection, the United States includes all areas under the jurisdiction of the United States including any of the places within the provisions of sections 5 and 7 of this title and section 46501(2) of title 49.

(f)

In the course of enforcement of subsection (a) and any other sections prohibiting a conspiracy or attempt to violate subsection (a), the Attorney General may request assistance from any Federal, State, or local agency, including the Army, Navy, and Air Force, any statute, rule, or regulation to the contrary, notwithstanding

Prev | Next

US CODE COLLECTION

search

TITLE **18** > **PART I** > **CHAPTER 7** > Sec. 113.

Prev | Next

Search this title:

[Search Title 18]

Notes
Updates
Parallel authorities
(CFR)
Topical references

Sec. 113. - Assaults within maritime and territorial jurisdiction

(a)

Whoever, within the special maritime and territorial jurisdiction of the United States, is guilty of an assault shall be punished as follows:

(1)

Assault with intent to commit murder, by imprisonment for not more than twenty years.

(2)

Assault with intent to commit any felony, except murder or a felony under chapter 109A, by a fine under this title or imprisonment for not more than ten years, or both.

(3)

Assault with a dangerous weapon, with intent to do bodily harm, and without just cause or excuse, by a fine under this title or imprisonment for not more than ten years, or both.

(4)

Assault by striking, beating, or wounding, by a fine under this title or imprisonment for not more than six months, or both.

(5)

Simple assault, by a fine under this title or imprisonment for not more than six months, or both, or if the victim of the assault is an individual who has not attained the age of 16 years, by fine under this title or imprisonment for not more than 1 year, or both.

(6)

Assault resulting in serious bodily injury, by a fine under this title or imprisonment for not more than ten years, or both.

(7)

Assault resulting in substantial bodily injury to an individual who has not attained the age of 16 years, by fine under this title or imprisonment for not more than 5 years, or both.

(b)

As used in this subsection -

(1)

the term "substantial bodily injury" means bodily injury which involves -

(A)

a temporary but substantial disfigurement; or

(B)

a temporary but substantial loss or impairment of the function of any bodily member, organ, or mental faculty; and

(2)

the term "serious bodily injury" has the meaning given that term in section 1365 of this title

Prev | Next

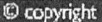

US CODE COLLECTION

search

Search this title:

Search Title 18

Notes
Updates
Parallel authorities
(CFR)
Topical references

Sec. 114. - Maiming within maritime and territorial jurisdiction

Whoever, within the special maritime and territorial jurisdiction of the United States, and with intent to torture (as defined in section 2340), maim, or disfigure, cuts, bites, or slits the nose, ear, or lip, or cuts out or disables the tongue, or puts out or destroys an eye, or cuts off or disables a limb or any member of another person; or

Whoever, within the special maritime and territorial jurisdiction of the United States, and with like intent, throws or pours upon another person, any scalding water, corrosive acid, or caustic substance -

Shall be fined under this title or imprisoned not more than twenty years, or both

© copyright   about us   send email

legal information institute

collection home

US CODE COLLECTION

search

TITLE 18 > PART I > CHAPTER 7 > Sec. 115.

Prev | Next

Sec. 115. - Influencing, impeding, or retaliating against a Federal official by threatening or injuring a family member

(a)

  (1)

    Whoever -

  (A)

    assaults, kidnaps, or murders, or attempts or conspires to kidnap or murder, or threatens to assault, kidnap or murder a member of the immediate family of a United States official, a United States judge, a Federal law enforcement officer, or an official whose killing would be a crime under section 1114 of this title; or

  (B)

    threatens to assault, kidnap, or murder, a United States official, a United States judge, a Federal law enforcement officer, or an official whose killing would be a crime under such section,

with intent to impede, intimidate, or interfere with such official, judge, or law enforcement officer while engaged in the performance of official duties, or with intent to retaliate against such official, judge, or law enforcement officer on account of the performance of official duties, shall be punished as provided in subsection (b).

  (2)

    Whoever assaults, kidnaps, or murders, or attempts or conspires to kidnap or murder, or threatens to assault, kidnap, or murder, any person who formerly served as a person designated in paragraph (1), or a member of the immediate family of any person who formerly served as a person designated in paragraph (1), with intent to

Search this title:

Search Title 18

Notes
Updates
Parallel authorities (CFR)
Topical references

retaliate against such person on account of the performance of official duties during the term of service of such person, shall be punished as provided in subsection (b).

(b)

(1)

An assault in violation of this section shall be punished as provided in section 111 of this title.

(2)

A kidnapping, attempted kidnapping, or conspiracy to kidnap in violation of this section shall be punished as provided in section 1201 of this title for the kidnapping, attempted kidnapping, or conspiracy to kidnap of a person described in section 1201(a)(5) of this title.

(3)

A murder, attempted murder, or conspiracy to murder in violation of this section shall be punished as provided in sections 1111, 1113, and 1117 of this title.

(4)

A threat made in violation of this section shall be punished by a fine under this title or imprisonment for a term of not more than five years, or both, except that imprisonment for a threatened assault shall not exceed three years.

(c)

As used in this section, the term -

(1)

"Federal law enforcement officer" means any officer, agent, or employee of the United States authorized by law or by a Government agency to engage in or supervise the prevention, detection, investigation, or prosecution of any violation of Federal criminal law;

(2)

"immediate family member" of an individual means -

(A)

his spouse, parent, brother or sister, child or person to whom he stands in loco parentis; or

(B)

any other person living in his household and related to him by blood or marriage;

(3)

"United States judge" means any judicial officer of the United States, and includes a justice of the Supreme Court and a United States magistrate judge; and

(4)

"United States official" means the President, President-elect, Vice President, Vice President-elect, a Member of Congress, a member-elect of Congress, a member of the executive branch who is the head of a department listed in 5 U.S.C. 101, or the Director of the Central Intelligence Agency.

(d)

This section shall not interfere with the investigative authority of the United States Secret Service, as provided under sections 3056, 871, and 879 of this title

Prev | Next

US CODE COLLECTION

search

TITLE 18 > PART I > CHAPTER 11B > Sec. 229.

Next

Sec. 229. - Prohibited activities

(a) Unlawful Conduct. -

Except as provided in subsection (b), it shall be unlawful for any person knowingly -

(1)

to develop, produce, otherwise acquire, transfer directly or indirectly, receive, stockpile, retain, own, possess, or use, or threaten to use, any chemical weapon; or

(2)

to assist or induce, in any way, any person to violate paragraph (1), or to attempt or conspire to violate paragraph (1).

(b) Exempted Agencies and Persons. -

(1) In general. -

Subsection (a) does not apply to the retention, ownership, possession, transfer, or receipt of a chemical weapon by a department, agency, or other entity of the United States, or by a person described in paragraph (2), pending destruction of the weapon.

(2) Exempted persons. -

A person referred to in paragraph (1) is -

(A)

any person, including a member of the Armed Forces of the United States, who is authorized by law or by an appropriate officer of the United States to retain, own, possess, transfer, or receive the chemical

Search this title:

Search Title 18

Notes
Updates
Parallel authorities (CFR)
Topical references

weapon; or

(B)

in an emergency situation, any otherwise nonculpable person if the person is attempting to destroy or seize the weapon.

(c) Jurisdiction. -

Conduct prohibited by subsection (a) is within the jurisdiction of the United States if the prohibited conduct -

(1)

takes place in the United States;

(2)

takes place outside of the United States and is committed by a national of the United States;

(3)

is committed against a national of the United States while the national is outside the United States; or

(4)

is committed against any property that is owned, leased, or used by the United States or by any department or agency of the United States, whether the property is within or outside the United States

Next

legal information institute

US CODE COLLECTION

search

TITLE 18 > PART I > CHAPTER 13 > Sec. 242.

Prev | Next

Sec. 242. - Deprivation of rights under color of law

Whoever, under color of any law, statute, ordinance, regulation, or custom, willfully subjects any person in any State, Territory, Commonwealth, Possession, or District to the deprivation of any rights, privileges, or immunities secured or protected by the Constitution or laws of the United States, or to different punishments, pains, or penalties, on account of such person being an alien, or by reason of his color, or race, than are prescribed for the punishment of citizens, shall be fined under this title or imprisoned not more than one year, or both; and if bodily injury results from the acts committed in violation of this section or if such acts include the use, attempted use, or threatened use of a dangerous weapon, explosives, or fire, shall be fined under this title or imprisoned not more than ten years, or both; and if death results from the acts committed in violation of this section or if such acts include kidnapping or an attempt to kidnap, aggravated sexual abuse, or an attempt to commit aggravated sexual abuse, or an attempt to kill, shall be fined under this title, or imprisoned for any term of years or for life, or both, or may be sentenced to death

Search this title:

Search Title 18

Notes
Updates
Parallel authorities
(CFR)
Topical references

Prev | Next

US CODE COLLECTION

search

Prev | Next

Sec. 245. - Federally protected activities

(a)

(1)

Nothing in this section shall be construed as indicating an intent on the part of Congress to prevent any State, any possession or Commonwealth of the United States, or the District of Columbia, from exercising jurisdiction over any offense over which it would have jurisdiction in the absence of this section, nor shall anything in this section be construed as depriving State and local law enforcement authorities of responsibility for prosecuting acts that may be violations of this section and that are violations of State and local law. No prosecution of any offense described in this section shall be undertaken by the United States except upon the certification in writing of the Attorney General, the Deputy Attorney General, the Associate Attorney General, or any Assistant Attorney General specially designated by the Attorney General that in his judgment a prosecution by the United States is in the public interest and necessary to secure substantial justice, which function of certification may not be delegated.

(2)

Nothing in this subsection shall be construed to limit the authority of Federal officers, or a Federal grand jury, to investigate possible violations of this section.

(b)

Whoever, whether or not acting under color of law, by force or threat of force willfully injures, intimidates or interferes with, or attempts to injure, intimidate or interfere with -

(1)

any person because he is or has been, or in order to

Search this title:

Search Title 18

Notes
Updates
Parallel authorities
(CFR)
Topical references

intimidate such person or any other person or any class of persons from -

(A)

voting or qualifying to vote, qualifying or campaigning as a candidate for elective office, or qualifying or acting as a poll watcher, or any legally authorized election official, in any primary, special, or general election;

(B)

participating in or enjoying any benefit, service, privilege, program, facility, or activity provided or administered by the United States;

(C)

applying for or enjoying employment, or any perquisite thereof, by any agency of the United States;

(D)

serving, or attending upon any court in connection with possible service, as a grand or petit juror in any court of the United States;

(E)

participating in or enjoying the benefits of any program or activity receiving Federal financial assistance; or

(2)

any person because of his race, color, religion or national origin and because he is or has been -

(A)

enrolling in or attending any public school or public college;

(B)

participating in or enjoying any benefit, service, privilege, program, facility or activity provided or administered by any State or subdivision thereof;

(C)

applying for or enjoying employment, or any perquisite thereof, by any private employer or any agency of any State or subdivision thereof, or joining or using the services or advantages of any labor organization, hiring hall, or employment agency;

(D)

serving, or attending upon any court of any State in connection with possible service, as a grand or petit juror;

(E)

traveling in or using any facility of interstate commerce, or using any vehicle, terminal, or facility of any common carrier by motor, rail, water, or air;

(F)

enjoying the goods, services, facilities, privileges, advantages, or accommodations of any inn, hotel, motel, or other establishment which provides lodging to transient guests, or of any restaurant, cafeteria, lunchroom, lunch counter, soda fountain, or other facility which serves the public and which is principally engaged in selling food or beverages for consumption on the premises, or of any gasoline station, or of any motion picture house, theater, concert hall, sports arena, stadium, or any other place of exhibition or entertainment which serves the public, or of any other establishment which serves the public and

(i)

which is located within the premises of any of the aforesaid establishments or within the premises of which is physically located any of the aforesaid establishments, and

(ii)

which holds itself out as serving patrons of such establishments; or

(3)

during or incident to a riot or civil disorder, any person engaged in a business in commerce or affecting commerce, including, but not limited to, any person engaged in a business which sells or offers for sale to interstate travelers a substantial portion of the articles, commodities, or services which it sells or where a substantial portion of the articles or commodities which it sells or offers for sale have moved in commerce; or

(4)

any person because he is or has been, or in order to intimidate such person or any other person or any class of persons from -

(A)

participating, without discrimination on account of race, color, religion or national origin, in any of the benefits or activities described in subparagraphs (1)(A) through (1)(E) or subparagraphs (2)(A) through (2)(F); or

(B)

affording another person or class of persons opportunity or protection to so participate; or

(5)

any citizen because he is or has been, or in order to intimidate such citizen or any other citizen from lawfully aiding or encouraging other persons to participate, without discrimination on account of race, color, religion or national origin, in any of the benefits or activities described in subparagraphs (1)(A) through (1)(E) or subparagraphs (2)(A) through (2)(F), or participating lawfully in speech or peaceful assembly opposing any denial of the opportunity to so participate - shall be fined under this title, or imprisoned not more than one year, or both; and if bodily injury results from the acts committed in violation of this section or if such acts include the use, attempted use, or threatened use of a dangerous weapon, explosives, or fire shall be fined under this title, or imprisoned not more than ten years, or both; and if death results from the acts committed in violation of this section or if such acts include kidnapping or an attempt to kidnap, aggravated sexual abuse or an attempt to commit aggravated sexual abuse, or an attempt to kill, shall be fined under this title or imprisoned for any term of years or for life, or both, or may be sentenced to death. As used in this section, the term "participating lawfully in speech or peaceful assembly" shall not mean the aiding, abetting, or inciting of other persons to riot or to commit any act of physical violence upon any individual or against any real or personal property in furtherance of a riot. Nothing in subparagraph (2)(F) or (4)(A) of this subsection shall apply to the proprietor of any establishment which provides lodging to transient guests, or to any employee acting on behalf of such proprietor, with respect to the enjoyment of the goods, services, facilities, privileges, advantages, or accommodations of such establishment if such establishment is located within a building which contains not more than five rooms for rent or hire and which is actually occupied by the proprietor as his residence.

(c)

Nothing in this section shall be construed so as to deter any law enforcement officer from lawfully carrying out the duties of his office; and no law enforcement officer shall be considered to be in violation of this section for lawfully carrying out the duties of his office or lawfully enforcing ordinances and laws of the United States, the District of Columbia, any of the several States, or any political subdivision of a State. For purposes of the preceding sentence, the term "law enforcement officer" means any officer of the United States, the District of Columbia, a State, or political subdivision of a State, who is empowered by law to conduct investigations of, or make arrests because of, offenses against the United States, the District of Columbia, a State, or a political subdivision of a State.

(d)

For purposes of this section, the term "State" includes a State of the United States, the District of Columbia, and any commonwealth, territory, or possession of the United States

Prev | Next

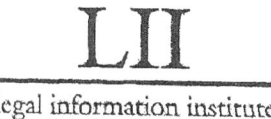

legal information institute

collection home

US CODE COLLECTION

search

TITLE 18 > PART I > CHAPTER 13 > Sec. 247.

Prev | Next

Sec. 247. - Damage to religious property; obstruction of persons in the free exercise of religious beliefs

(a)

Whoever, in any of the circumstances referred to in subsection (b) of this section -

(1)

intentionally defaces, damages, or destroys any religious real property, because of the religious character of that property, or attempts to do so; or

(2)

intentionally obstructs, by force or threat of force, any person in the enjoyment of that person's free exercise of religious beliefs, or attempts to do so;

shall be punished as provided in subsection (d).

(b)

The circumstances referred to in subsection (a) are that the offense is in or affects interstate or foreign commerce.

(c)

Whoever intentionally defaces, damages, or destroys any religious real property because of the race, color, or ethnic characteristics of any individual associated with that religious property, or attempts to do so, shall be punished as provided in subsection (d).

(d)

The punishment for a violation of subsection (a) of this section shall be -

(1)

Search this title:

Search Title 18

Notes
Updates
Parallel authorities (CFR)
Topical references

if death results from acts committed in violation of this section or if such acts include kidnapping or an attempt to kidnap, aggravated sexual abuse or an attempt to commit aggravated sexual abuse, or an attempt to kill, a fine in accordance with this title and imprisonment for any term of years or for life, or both, or may be sentenced to death;

(2)

if bodily injury results to any person, including any public safety officer performing duties as a direct or proximate result of conduct prohibited by this section, and the violation is by means of fire or an explosive, a fine under this title or imprisonment for not more that 40 years, or both;

(3)

if bodily injury to any person, including any public safety officer performing duties as a direct or proximate result of conduct prohibited by this section, results from the acts committed in violation of this section or if such acts include the use, attempted use, or threatened use of a dangerous weapon, explosives, or fire, a fine in accordance with this title and imprisonment for not more than 20 years, or both; and

(4)

in any other case, a fine in accordance with this title and imprisonment for not more than one year, or both.

(e)

No prosecution of any offense described in this section shall be undertaken by the United States except upon the certification in writing of the Attorney General or his designee that in his judgment a prosecution by the United States is in the public interest and necessary to secure substantial justice.

(f)

As used in this section, the term "religious real property" means any church, synagogue, mosque, religious cemetery, or other religious real property, including fixtures or religious objects contained within a place of religious worship.

(g)

No person shall be prosecuted, tried, or punished for any noncapital offense under this section unless the indictment is found or the information is instituted not later than 7 years after the date on which the offense was committed

Prev | Next

© copyright   about us   send email

search

Prev

Search this title:

[   ]

Search Title 18

Notes
Updates
Parallel authorities
(CFR)
Topical references

Sec. 248. - Freedom of access to clinic entrances

(a) Prohibited Activities. -

Whoever -

(1)

by force or threat of force or by physical obstruction, intentionally injures, intimidates or interferes with or attempts to injure, intimidate or interfere with any person because that person is or has been, or in order to intimidate such person or any other person or any class of persons from, obtaining or providing reproductive health services;

(2)

by force or threat of force or by physical obstruction, intentionally injures, intimidates or interferes with or attempts to injure, intimidate or interfere with any person lawfully exercising or seeking to exercise the First Amendment right of religious freedom at a place of religious worship; or

(3)

intentionally damages or destroys the property of a facility, or attempts to do so, because such facility provides reproductive health services, or intentionally damages or destroys the property of a place of religious worship,

shall be subject to the penalties provided in subsection (b) and the civil remedies provided in subsection (c), except that a parent or legal guardian of a minor shall not be subject to any penalties or civil remedies under this section for such activities insofar as they are directed exclusively at that minor.

(b) Penalties. -

Whoever violates this section shall -

(1)

in the case of a first offense, be fined in accordance with this title, or imprisoned not more than one year, or both; and

(2)

in the case of a second or subsequent offense after a prior conviction under this section, be fined in accordance with this title, or imprisoned not more than 3 years, or both;

except that for an offense involving exclusively a nonviolent physical obstruction, the fine shall be not more than $10,000 and the length of imprisonment shall be not more than six months, or both, for the first offense; and the fine shall, notwithstanding section 3571, be not more than $25,000 and the length of imprisonment shall be not more than 18 months, or both, for a subsequent offense; and except that if bodily injury results, the length of imprisonment shall be not more than 10 years, and if death results, it shall be for any term of years or for life.

(c) Civil Remedies. -

(1) Right of action. -

(A) In general. -

Any person aggrieved by reason of the conduct prohibited by subsection (a) may commence a civil action for the relief set forth in subparagraph (B), except that such an action may be brought under subsection (a)(1) only by a person involved in providing or seeking to provide, or obtaining or seeking to obtain, services in a facility that provides reproductive health services, and such an action may be brought under subsection (a)(2) only by a person lawfully exercising or seeking to exercise the First Amendment right of religious freedom at a place of religious worship or by the entity that owns or operates such place of religious worship.

(B) Relief. -

In any action under subparagraph (A), the court may award appropriate relief, including temporary, preliminary or permanent injunctive relief and compensatory and punitive damages, as well as the costs of suit and reasonable fees for attorneys and expert witnesses. With respect to compensatory damages, the plaintiff may elect, at any time prior to the rendering of final judgment, to recover, in lieu of actual damages, an award of statutory damages in the amount of $5,000 per violation.

(2) Action by attorney general of the united states. -

    (A) In general. -

        If the Attorney General of the United States has reasonable cause to believe that any person or group of persons is being, has been, or may be injured by conduct constituting a violation of this section, the Attorney General may commence a civil action in any appropriate United States District Court.

    (B) Relief. -

        In any action under subparagraph (A), the court may award appropriate relief, including temporary, preliminary or permanent injunctive relief, and compensatory damages to persons aggrieved as described in paragraph (1)(B). The court, to vindicate the public interest, may also assess a civil penalty against each respondent -

        (i)

            in an amount not exceeding $10,000 for a nonviolent physical obstruction and $15,000 for other first violations; and

        (ii)

            in an amount not exceeding $15,000 for a nonviolent physical obstruction and $25,000 for any other subsequent violation.

(3) Actions by state attorneys general. -

    (A) In general. -

        If the Attorney General of a State has reasonable cause to believe that any person or group of persons is being, has been, or may be injured by conduct constituting a violation of this section, such Attorney General may commence a civil action in the name of such State, as parens patriae on behalf of natural persons residing in such State, in any appropriate United States District Court.

(B) Relief. -

In any action under subparagraph (A), the court may award appropriate relief, including temporary, preliminary or permanent injunctive relief, compensatory damages, and civil penalties as described in paragraph (2)(B).

(d) Rules of Construction. -

Nothing in this section shall be construed -

(1)

to prohibit any expressive conduct (including peaceful picketing or other peaceful demonstration) protected from legal prohibition by the First Amendment to the Constitution;

(2)

to create new remedies for interference with activities protected by the free speech or free exercise clauses of the First Amendment to the Constitution, occurring outside a facility, regardless of the point of view expressed, or to limit any existing legal remedies for such interference;

(3)

to provide exclusive criminal penalties or civil remedies with respect to the conduct prohibited by this section, or to preempt State or local laws that may provide such penalties or remedies; or

(4)

to interfere with the enforcement of State or local laws regulating the performance of abortions or other reproductive health services.

(e) Definitions. -

As used in this section:

(1) Facility. -

The term "facility" includes a hospital, clinic,

physician's office, or other facility that provides reproductive health services, and includes the building or structure in which the facility is located.

(2) Interfere with. -

The term "interfere with" means to restrict a person's freedom of movement.

(3) Intimidate. -

The term "intimidate" means to place a person in reasonable apprehension of bodily harm to him- or herself or to another.

(4) Physical obstruction. -

The term "physical obstruction" means rendering impassable ingress to or egress from a facility that provides reproductive health services or to or from a place of religious worship, or rendering passage to or from such a facility or place of religious worship unreasonably difficult or hazardous.

(5) Reproductive health services. -

The term "reproductive health services" means reproductive health services provided in a hospital, clinic, physician's office, or other facility, and includes medical, surgical, counselling or referral services relating to the human reproductive system, including services relating to pregnancy or the termination of a pregnancy.

(6) State. -

The term "State" includes a State of the United States, the District of Columbia, and any commonwealth, territory, or possession of the United States.

Prev

US CODE COLLECTION

search

TITLE 18 > PART I > CHAPTER 18 > Sec. 351.

Sec. 351. - Congressional, Cabinet, and Supreme Court assassination, kidnapping, and assault; penalties

(a)

Whoever kills any individual who is a Member of Congress or a Member-of-Congress-elect, a member of the executive branch of the Government who is the head, or a person nominated to be head during the pendency of such nomination, of a department listed in section 101 of title 5 or the second ranking official in such department, the Director (or a person nominated to be Director during the pendency of such nomination) or Deputy Director of Central Intelligence, a major Presidential or Vice Presidential candidate (as defined in section 3056 of this title), or a Justice of the United States, as defined in section 451 of title 28, or a person nominated to be a Justice of the United States, during the pendency of such nomination, shall be punished as provided by sections 1111 and 1112 of this title.

(b)

Whoever kidnaps any individual designated in subsection (a) of this section shall be punished

(1)

by imprisonment for any term of years or for life, or

(2)

by death or imprisonment for any term of years or for life, if death results to such individual.

(c)

Whoever attempts to kill or kidnap any individual designated in subsection (a) of this section shall be punished by imprisonment for any term of years or for life.

Search this title:

Search Title 18

Notes
Updates
Parallel authorities (CFR)
Topical references

(d)

If two or more persons conspire to kill or kidnap any individual designated in subsection (a) of this section and one or more of such persons do any act to effect the object of the conspiracy, each shall be punished

(1)

by imprisonment for any term of years or for life, or

(2)

by death or imprisonment for any term of years or for life, if death results to such individual.

(e)

Whoever assaults any person designated in subsection (a) of this section shall be fined under this title, or imprisoned not more than one year, or both; and if the assault involved the use of a dangerous weapon, or personal injury results, shall be fined under this title, or imprisoned not more than ten years, or both.

(f)

If Federal investigative or prosecutive jurisdiction is asserted for a violation of this section, such assertion shall suspend the exercise of jurisdiction by a State or local authority, under any applicable State or local law, until Federal action is terminated.

(g)

Violations of this section shall be investigated by the Federal Bureau of Investigation. Assistance may be requested from any Federal, State, or local agency, including the Army, Navy, and Air Force, any statute, rule, or regulation to the contrary notwithstanding.

(h)

In a prosecution for an offense under this section the Government need not prove that the defendant knew that the victim of the offense was an individual protected by this section.

(i)

There is extraterritorial jurisdiction over the conduct prohibited by this section

US CODE COLLECTION

search

Search this title:

Search Title 18

Notes
Updates
Parallel authorities
(CFR)
Topical references

Sec. 831. - Prohibited transactions involving nuclear materials

(a)

Whoever, if one of the circumstances described in subsection (c) of this section occurs -

(1)

without lawful authority, intentionally receives, possesses, uses, transfers, alters, disposes of, or disperses any nuclear material or nuclear byproduct material and -

(A)

thereby knowingly causes the death of or serious bodily injury to any person or substantial damage to property or to the environment; or

(B)

circumstances exist, or have been represented to the defendant to exist, that are likely to cause the death or serious bodily injury to any person, or substantial damage to property or to the environment;

(2)

with intent to deprive another of nuclear material or nuclear byproduct material, knowingly -

(A)

takes and carries away nuclear material or nuclear byproduct material of another without authority;

(B)

makes an unauthorized use, disposition, or transfer, of nuclear material or nuclear byproduct material belonging to another; or

(C)

uses fraud and thereby obtains nuclear material or nuclear byproduct material belonging to another;

(3)

knowingly -

(A)

uses force; or

(B)

threatens or places another in fear that any person other than the actor will imminently be subject to bodily injury;

and thereby takes nuclear material or nuclear byproduct material belonging to another from the person or presence of any other;

(4)

intentionally intimidates any person and thereby obtains nuclear material or nuclear byproduct material belonging to another;

(5)

with intent to compel any person, international organization, or governmental entity to do or refrain from doing any act, knowingly threatens to engage in conduct described in paragraph (2)(A) or (3) of this subsection;

(6)

knowingly threatens to use nuclear material or nuclear byproduct material to cause death or serious bodily injury to any person or substantial damage to property or to the environment under circumstances in which the threat may reasonably be understood as an expression of serious purposes;

(7)

attempts to commit an offense under paragraph (1), (2), (3), or (4) of this subsection; or

(8)

is a party to a conspiracy of two or more persons to

commit an offense under paragraph (1), (2), (3), or (4) of this subsection, if any of the parties intentionally engages in any conduct in furtherance of such offense;

shall be punished as provided in subsection (b) of this section.

(b)

The punishment for an offense under -

(1)

paragraphs (1) through (7) of subsection (a) of this section is -

(A)

a fine under this title; and

(B)

imprisonment -

(i)

for any term of years or for life

(I)

if, while committing the offense, the offender knowingly causes the death of any person; or

(II)

if, while committing an offense under paragraph (1) or (3) of subsection (a) of this section, the offender, under circumstances manifesting extreme indifference to the life of an individual, knowingly engages in any conduct and thereby recklessly causes the death of or serious bodily injury to any person; and

(ii)

for not more than 20 years in any other case; and

(2)

paragraph (8) of subsection (a) of this section is -

(A)

a fine under this title; and

(B)

imprisonment -

(i)

for not more than 20 years if the offense which is the object of the conspiracy is punishable under paragraph (1)(B)(i); and

(ii)

for not more than 10 years in any other case.

(c)

The circumstances referred to in subsection (a) of this section are that -

(1)

the offense is committed in the United States or the special maritime and territorial jurisdiction of the United States, or the special aircraft jurisdiction of the United States (as defined in section 46501 of title 49);

(2)

an offender or a victim is -

(A)

a national of the United States; or

(B)

a United States corporation or other legal entity;

(3)

after the conduct required for the offense occurs the defendant is found in the United States, even if the conduct required for the offense occurs outside the United States;

(4)

the conduct required for the offense occurs with respect to the carriage of a consignment of nuclear material or nuclear byproduct material by any means of transportation intended to go beyond the territory of the state where the shipment originates beginning with the departure from a facility of the shipper in that state and ending with the arrival at a facility of the receiver within the state of ultimate destination and either of such states is the United States; or

(5)

either -

(A)

the governmental entity under subsection (a)(5) is the United States; or

(B)

the threat under subsection (a)(6) is directed at the United States.

(d)

The Attorney General may request assistance from the Secretary of Defense under chapter 18 of title 10 in the enforcement of this section and the Secretary of Defense may provide such assistance in accordance with chapter 18 of title 10, except that the Secretary of Defense may provide such assistance through any Department of Defense personnel.

(e)

(1)

The Attorney General may also request assistance from the Secretary of Defense under this subsection in the enforcement of this section. Notwithstanding section 1385 of this title, the Secretary of Defense may, in accordance with other applicable law, provide such assistance to the Attorney General if -

(A)

an emergency situation exists (as jointly determined by the Attorney General and the Secretary of Defense in their discretion); and

(B)

the provision of such assistance will not adversely affect the military preparedness of the United States (as determined by the Secretary of Defense in such Secretary's discretion).

(2)

As used in this subsection, the term "emergency situation" means a circumstance -

(A)

that poses a serious threat to the interests of the United States; and

(B)

in which -

(i)

enforcement of the law would be seriously impaired if the assistance were not provided; and

(ii)

civilian law enforcement personnel are not capable of enforcing the law.

(3)

Assistance under this section may include -

(A)

use of personnel of the Department of Defense to arrest persons and conduct searches and seizures with respect to violations of this section; and

(B)

such other activity as is incidental to the enforcement of this section, or to the protection of persons or property from conduct that violates this section.

(4)

The Secretary of Defense may require reimbursement as a condition of assistance under this section.

(5)

The Attorney General may delegate the Attorney General's function under this subsection only to a Deputy, Associate, or Assistant Attorney General.

(f)

As used in this section -

(1)

the term "nuclear material" means material containing any -

(A)

plutonium;

(B)

uranium not in the form of ore or ore residue that contains the mixture of isotopes as occurring in nature;

(C)

enriched uranium, defined as uranium that contains the isotope 233 or 235 or both in such amount that the abundance ratio of the sum of those isotopes to the isotope 238 is greater than the ratio of the isotope 235 to the isotope 238 occurring in nature; or

(D)

uranium 233;

(2)

the term ''nuclear byproduct material'' means any material containing any radioactive isotope created through an irradiation process in the operation of a nuclear reactor or accelerator;

(3)

the term ''international organization'' means a public international organization designated as such pursuant to section 1 of the International Organizations Immunities Act (22 U.S.C. 288) or a public organization created pursuant to treaty or other agreement under international law as an instrument through or by which two or more foreign governments engage in some aspect of their conduct of international affairs;

(4)

the term ''serious bodily injury'' means bodily injury which involves -

(A)

a substantial risk of death;

(B)

extreme physical pain;

(C)

protracted and obvious disfigurement; or

(D)

protracted loss or impairment of the function of a bodily member, organ, or mental faculty;

(5)

the term "bodily injury" means -

(A)

a cut, abrasion, bruise, burn, or disfigurement;

(B)

physical pain;

(C)

illness;

(D)

impairment of a function of a bodily member, organ, or mental faculty; or

(E)

any other injury to the body, no matter how temporary;

(6)

the term "national of the United States" has the same meaning as in section 101(a)(22) of the Immigration and Nationality Act (8 U.S.C. 1101(a)(22)); and

(7)

the term "United States corporation or other legal entity" means any corporation or other entity organized under the laws of the United States or any State, Commonwealth, territory, possession, or district of the United States

Next

US CODE COLLECTION

search

TITLE 18 > PART I > CHAPTER 40 > Sec. 844.

Prev | Next

Sec. 844. - Penalties

(a)

> Any person who -

> **(1)**

>> violates any of subsections (a) through (i) or (l) through (o) of section 842 shall be fined under this title, imprisoned for not more than 10 years, or both; and

> **(2)**

>> violates subsection (p)(2) of section 842, shall be fined under this title, imprisoned not more than 20 years, or both.

(b)

> Any person who violates any other provision of section 842 of this chapter shall be fined under this title or imprisoned not more than one year, or both.

(c)

> **(1)**

>> Any explosive materials involved or used or intended to be used in any violation of the provisions of this chapter or any other rule or regulation promulgated thereunder or any violation of any criminal law of the United States shall be subject to seizure and forfeiture, and all provisions of the Internal Revenue Code of 1986 relating to the seizure, forfeiture, and disposition of firearms, as defined in section 5845(a) of that Code, shall, so far as applicable, extend to seizures and forfeitures under the provisions of this chapter.

> **(2)**

>> Notwithstanding paragraph (1), in the case of the

Search this title:

Search Title 18

Notes
Updates
Parallel authorities
(CFR)
Topical references

seizure of any explosive materials for any offense for which the materials would be subject to forfeiture in which it would be impracticable or unsafe to remove the materials to a place of storage or would be unsafe to store them, the seizing officer may destroy the explosive materials forthwith. Any destruction under this paragraph shall be in the presence of at least 1 credible witness. The seizing officer shall make a report of the seizure and take samples as the Secretary may by regulation prescribe.

(3)

Within 60 days after any destruction made pursuant to paragraph (2), the owner of (including any person having an interest in) the property so destroyed may make application to the Secretary for reimbursement of the value of the property. If the claimant establishes to the satisfaction of the Secretary that -

(A)

the property has not been used or involved in a violation of law; or

(B)

any unlawful involvement or use of the property was without the claimant's knowledge, consent, or willful blindness,

the Secretary shall make an allowance to the claimant not exceeding the value of the property destroyed.

(d)

Whoever transports or receives, or attempts to transport or receive, in interstate or foreign commerce any explosive with the knowledge or intent that it will be used to kill, injure, or intimidate any individual or unlawfully to damage or destroy any building, vehicle, or other real or personal property, shall be imprisoned for not more than ten years, or fined under this title, or both; and if personal injury results to any person, including any public safety officer performing duties as a direct or proximate result of conduct prohibited by this subsection, shall be imprisoned for not more than twenty years or fined under this title, or both; and if death results to any person, including any public safety officer performing duties as a direct or proximate result of conduct prohibited by this subsection, shall be subject to imprisonment for any term of years, or to the death penalty or to life imprisonment.

(e)

Whoever, through the use of the mail, telephone, telegraph, or other instrument of interstate or foreign commerce, or in or affecting interstate or foreign commerce, willfully makes any threat, or maliciously conveys false information knowing the same to be false, concerning an attempt or alleged attempt being made, or to be made, to kill, injure, or intimidate any individual or unlawfully to damage or destroy any building, vehicle, or other real or personal property by means of fire or an explosive shall be imprisoned for not more than 10 years or fined under this title, or both.

(f)

(1)

Whoever maliciously damages or destroys, or attempts to damage or destroy, by means of fire or an explosive, any building, vehicle, or other personal or real property in whole or in part owned or possessed by, or leased to, the United States, or any department or agency thereof, shall be imprisoned for not less than 5 years and not more than 20 years, fined under this title, or both.

(2)

Whoever engages in conduct prohibited by this subsection, and as a result of such conduct, directly or proximately causes personal injury or creates a substantial risk of injury to any person, including any public safety officer performing duties, shall be imprisoned for not less than 7 years and not more than 40 years, fined under this title, or both.

(3)

Whoever engages in conduct prohibited by this subsection, and as a result of such conduct directly or proximately causes the death of any person, including any public safety officer performing duties, shall be subject to the death penalty, or imprisoned for not less than 20 years or for life, fined under this title, or both.

(g)

(1)

Except as provided in paragraph (2), whoever possesses an explosive in an airport that is subject to the regulatory authority of the Federal Aviation Administration, or in any building in whole or in part owned, possessed, or used by, or leased to, the United States or any department or agency thereof, except with the written consent of the agency, department, or other person responsible for the management of such building or airport, shall be imprisoned for not more than five years, or fined under this title, or both.

(2)

The provisions of this subsection shall not be applicable to -

(A)

the possession of ammunition (as that term is defined in regulations issued pursuant to this chapter) in an airport that is subject to the regulatory authority of the Federal Aviation Administration if such ammunition is either in checked baggage or in a closed container; or

(B)

the possession of an explosive in an airport if the packaging and transportation of such explosive is exempt from, or subject to and in accordance with, regulations of the Research and Special Projects Administration for the handling of hazardous materials pursuant to chapter 51 of title 49.

(h)

Whoever -

(1)

uses fire or an explosive to commit any felony which may be prosecuted in a court of the United States, or

(2)

carries an explosive during the commission of any felony which may be prosecuted in a court of the United States,

including a felony which provides for an enhanced punishment if committed by the use of a deadly or dangerous weapon or device shall, in addition to the punishment provided for such felony, be sentenced to imprisonment for 10 years. In the case of a second or subsequent conviction under this subsection, such person shall be sentenced to imprisonment for 20 years. Notwithstanding any other provision of law, the court shall not place on probation or suspend the sentence of any person convicted of a violation of this subsection, nor shall the term of imprisonment imposed under this subsection run concurrently with any other term of imprisonment including that imposed for the felony in which the explosive was used or carried.

(i)

Whoever maliciously damages or destroys, or attempts to damage or destroy, by means of fire or an explosive, any building, vehicle, or other real or personal property used in interstate or foreign commerce or in any activity affecting interstate or foreign commerce shall be imprisoned for not less than 5 years and not more than 20 years, fined under this title, or both; and if personal injury results to any person, including any public safety officer performing duties as a direct or proximate result of conduct prohibited by this subsection, shall be imprisoned for not less than 7 years and not more than 40 years, fined under this title, or both; and if death results to any person, including any public safety officer performing duties as a direct or proximate result of conduct prohibited by this subsection, shall also be subject to imprisonment for any term of years, or to the death penalty or to life imprisonment.

(j)

For the purposes of subsections (d), (e), (f), (g), (h), and (i) of this section and section 842(p), the term "explosive" means gunpowders, powders used for blasting, all forms of high explosives, blasting materials, fuzes (other than electric circuit breakers), detonators, and other detonating agents, smokeless powders, other explosive or incendiary devices within the meaning of paragraph (5) of section 232 of this title, and any chemical compounds, mechanical mixture, or device that contains any oxidizing and combustible units, or other ingredients, in such proportions, quantities, or packing that ignition by fire, by friction, by concussion, by percussion, or by detonation of the compound, mixture, or device or any part thereof may cause an explosion.

(k)

A person who steals any explosives materials which are moving as, or are a part of, or which have moved in, interstate or foreign commerce shall be imprisoned for not more than 10 years, fined under this title, or both.

(l)

A person who steals any explosive material from a licensed importer, licensed manufacturer, or licensed dealer, or from any permittee shall be fined under this title, imprisoned not more than 10 years, or both.

(m)

A person who conspires to commit an offense under subsection (h) shall be imprisoned for any term of years not exceeding 20, fined under this title, or both.

(n)

Except as otherwise provided in this section, a person who conspires to commit any offense defined in this chapter shall be subject to the same penalties (other than the penalty of death) as the penalties prescribed for the offense the commission of which was the object of the conspiracy.

(o)

Whoever knowingly transfers any explosive materials, knowing or having reasonable cause to believe that such explosive materials will be used to commit a crime of violence (as defined in section 924(c)(3)) or drug trafficking crime (as defined in section 924(c)(2)) shall be subject to the same penalties as may be imposed under subsection (h) for a first conviction for the use or carrying of an explosive material

Prev | Next

US CODE COLLECTION

Prev | Next

Sec. 924. - Penalties

(a)

(1)

Except as otherwise provided in this subsection, subsection (b), (c), or (f) of this section, or in section 929, whoever -

(A)

knowingly makes any false statement or representation with respect to the information required by this chapter to be kept in the records of a person licensed under this chapter or in applying for any license or exemption or relief from disability under the provisions of this chapter;

(B)

knowingly violates subsection (a)(4), (f), (k), (r), (v), or (w) of section 922;

(C)

knowingly imports or brings into the United States or any possession thereof any firearm or ammunition in violation of section 922(l); or

(D)

willfully violates any other provision of this chapter,

shall be fined under this title, imprisoned not more than five years, or both.

(2)

Whoever knowingly violates subsection (a)(6), (d), (g), (h), (i), (j), or (o) of section 922 shall be fined as provided in this title, imprisoned not more than 10 years, or both.

(3)

Any licensed dealer, licensed importer, licensed manufacturer, or licensed collector who knowingly -

(A)

makes any false statement or representation with respect to the information required by the provisions of this chapter to be kept in the records of a person licensed under this chapter, or

(B)

violates subsection (m) of section 922,

shall be fined under this title, imprisoned not more than one year, or both.

(4)

Whoever violates section 922(q) shall be fined under this title, imprisoned for not more than 5 years, or both. Notwithstanding any other provision of law, the term of imprisonment imposed under this paragraph shall not run concurrently with any other term of imprisonment imposed under any other provision of law. Except for the authorization of a term of imprisonment of not more than 5 years made in this paragraph, for the purpose of any other law a violation of section 922(q) shall be deemed to be a misdemeanor.

(5)

Whoever knowingly violates subsection (s) or (t) of section 922 shall be fined under this title, imprisoned for not more than 1 year, or both.

(6)

(A)

(i)

A juvenile who violates section 922(x) shall be fined under this title, imprisoned not more than 1 year, or both, except that a juvenile described in clause (ii) shall be sentenced to probation on appropriate conditions and shall not be incarcerated unless the juvenile fails to comply with a condition of probation.

(ii)

A juvenile is described in this clause if -

(I)

the offense of which the juvenile is charged is possession of a handgun or ammunition in violation of section 922(x)(2); and

(II)

the juvenile has not been convicted in any court of an offense (including an offense under section 922(x) or a similar State law, but not including any other offense consisting of conduct that if engaged in by an adult would not constitute an offense) or adjudicated as a juvenile delinquent for conduct that if engaged in by an adult would constitute an offense.

(B)

A person other than a juvenile who knowingly violates section 922(x) -

(i)

shall be fined under this title, imprisoned not more than 1 year, or both; and

(ii)

if the person sold, delivered, or otherwise transferred a handgun or ammunition to a juvenile knowing or having reasonable cause to know that the juvenile intended to carry or otherwise possess or discharge or otherwise use the handgun or ammunition in the commission of a crime of violence, shall be fined under this title, imprisoned not more than 10 years, or both.

(b)

Whoever, with intent to commit therewith an offense punishable by imprisonment for a term exceeding one year, or with knowledge or reasonable cause to believe that an offense punishable by imprisonment for a term exceeding one year is to be committed therewith, ships, transports, or receives a firearm or any ammunition in interstate or foreign commerce shall be fined under this title, or imprisoned not more than ten years, or both.

(c)

(1)

(A)

Except to the extent that a greater minimum sentence is otherwise provided by this subsection or by any other provision of law, any person who, during and in relation to any crime of violence or drug trafficking crime (including a crime of violence or drug trafficking crime that provides for an enhanced punishment if committed by the use of a deadly or dangerous weapon or device) for which the person may be prosecuted in a court of the United States, uses or carries a firearm, or who, in furtherance of any such crime, possesses a firearm, shall, in addition to the punishment provided for such crime of violence or drug trafficking crime -

(i)

be sentenced to a term of imprisonment of not less than 5 years;

(ii)

if the firearm is brandished, be sentenced to a term of imprisonment of not less than 7 years; and

(iii)

if the firearm is discharged, be sentenced to a term of imprisonment of not less than 10 years.

(B)

If the firearm possessed by a person convicted of a violation of this subsection -

(i)

is a short-barreled rifle, short-barreled shotgun, or semiautomatic assault weapon, the person shall be sentenced to a term of imprisonment of not less than 10 years; or

(ii)

is a machinegun or a destructive device, or is equipped with a firearm silencer or firearm muffler, the person shall be sentenced to a term of imprisonment of not less than 30 years.

(C)

In the case of a second or subsequent conviction under this subsection, the person shall -

(i)

be sentenced to a term of imprisonment of not less than 25 years; and

(ii)

if the firearm involved is a machinegun or a destructive device, or is equipped with a firearm silencer or firearm muffler, be sentenced to imprisonment for life.

(D)

Notwithstanding any other provision of law -

(i)

a court shall not place on probation any person convicted of a violation of this subsection; and

(ii)

no term of imprisonment imposed on a person under this subsection shall run concurrently with any other term of imprisonment imposed on the person, including any term of imprisonment imposed for the crime of violence or drug trafficking crime during which the firearm was used, carried, or possessed.

(2)

For purposes of this subsection, the term "drug trafficking crime" means any felony punishable under the Controlled Substances Act (21 U.S.C. 801 et seq.), the Controlled Substances Import and Export Act (21 U.S.C. 951 et seq.), or the Maritime Drug Law Enforcement Act (46 U.S.C. App. 1901 et seq.).

(3)

For purposes of this subsection the term "crime of violence" means an offense that is a felony and -

(A)

has as an element the use, attempted use, or threatened use of physical force against the person or property of another, or

(B)

that by its nature, involves a substantial risk that physical force against the person or property of another may be used in the course of committing the offense.

(4)

For purposes of this subsection, the term "brandish" means, with respect to a firearm, to display all or part of the firearm, or otherwise make the presence of the firearm known to another person, in order to intimidate that person, regardless of whether the firearm is directly visible to that person.

(d)

(1)

Any firearm or ammunition involved in or used in any knowing violation of subsection (a)(4), (a)(6), (f), (g), (h), (i), (j), or (k) of section 922, or knowing importation or bringing into the United States or any possession thereof any firearm or ammunition in violation of section 922(l), or knowing violation of section 924, or willful violation of any other provision of this chapter or any rule or regulation promulgated thereunder, or any violation of any other criminal law of the United States, or any firearm or ammunition intended to be used in any offense referred to in paragraph (3) of this subsection, where such intent is demonstrated by clear and convincing evidence, shall be subject to seizure and forfeiture, and all provisions of the Internal Revenue Code of 1986 relating to the seizure, forfeiture, and disposition of firearms, as defined in section 5845(a) of that Code, shall, so far as applicable, extend to seizures and forfeitures under the provisions of this chapter: Provided, That upon acquittal of the owner or possessor, or dismissal of the charges against him other than upon motion of the Government prior to trial, or lapse of or court termination of the restraining order to which he is subject, the seized or relinquished firearms or ammunition shall be returned forthwith to the owner or possessor or to a person delegated by the owner or possessor unless the return of the firearms or ammunition would place the owner or possessor or his delegate in violation of law. Any action or proceeding for the forfeiture of firearms or ammunition shall be commenced within one hundred and twenty days of such seizure.

(2)

(A)

In any action or proceeding for the return of firearms or ammunition seized under the provisions of this chapter, the court shall allow the prevailing party, other than the United States, a reasonable attorney's fee, and the United States shall be liable therefor.

(B)

In any other action or proceeding under the provisions of this chapter, the court, when it finds that such action was without foundation, or was initiated vexatiously, frivolously, or in bad faith, shall allow the prevailing party, other than the United States, a reasonable attorney's fee, and the United States shall be liable therefor.

(C)

Only those firearms or quantities of ammunition particularly named and individually identified as involved in or used in any violation of the provisions of this chapter or any rule or regulation issued thereunder, or any other criminal law of the United States or as intended to be used in any offense referred to in paragraph (3) of this subsection, where such intent is demonstrated by clear and convincing evidence, shall be subject to seizure, forfeiture, and disposition.

(D)

The United States shall be liable for attorneys' fees under this paragraph only to the extent provided in advance by appropriation Acts.

(3)

The offenses referred to in paragraphs (1) and (2)(C) of this subsection are -

(A)

any crime of violence, as that term is defined in section 924(c)(3) of this title;

(B)

any offense punishable under the Controlled Substances Act (21 U.S.C. 801 et seq.) or the Controlled Substances Import and Export Act (21 U.S.C. 951 et seq.);

(C)

any offense described in section 922(a)(1), 922(a)

(3), 922(a)(5), or 922(b)(3) of this title, where the firearm or ammunition intended to be used in any such offense is involved in a pattern of activities which includes a violation of any offense described in section 922(a)(1), 922(a)(3), 922(a)(5), or 922(b)(3) of this title;

(D)

any offense described in section 922(d) of this title where the firearm or ammunition is intended to be used in such offense by the transferor of such firearm or ammunition;

(E)

any offense described in section 922(i), 922(j), 922(l), 922(n), or 924(b) of this title; and

(F)

any offense which may be prosecuted in a court of the United States which involves the exportation of firearms or ammunition.

(e)

(1)

In the case of a person who violates section 922(g) of this title and has three previous convictions by any court referred to in section 922(g)(1) of this title for a violent felony or a serious drug offense, or both, committed on occasions different from one another, such person shall be fined not more than $25,000 and imprisoned not less than fifteen years, and, notwithstanding any other provision of law, the court shall not suspend the sentence of, or grant a probationary sentence to, such person with respect to the conviction under section 922(g).

(2)

As used in this subsection -

(A)

the term "serious drug offense" means -

(i)

an offense under the Controlled Substances Act (21 U.S.C. 801 et seq.), the Controlled Substances Import and Export Act (21 U.S.C. 951 et seq.), or the Maritime Drug Law Enforcement Act (46 U.S.C. App. 1901 et seq.) for which a maximum term of imprisonment of ten years or more is prescribed by law; or

(ii)

an offense under State law, involving manufacturing, distributing, or possessing with intent to manufacture or distribute, a controlled substance (as defined in section 102 of the Controlled Substances Act (21 U.S.C. 802)), for which a maximum term of imprisonment of ten years or more is prescribed by law;

(B)

the term "violent felony" means any crime punishable by imprisonment for a term exceeding one year, or any act of juvenile delinquency involving the use or carrying of a firearm, knife, or destructive device that would be punishable by imprisonment for such term if committed by an adult, that -

(i)

has as an element the use, attempted use, or threatened use of physical force against the person of another; or

(ii)

is burglary, arson, or extortion, involves use of explosives, or otherwise involves conduct that presents a serious potential risk of physical injury to another; and

(C)

the term "conviction" includes a finding that a person has committed an act of juvenile delinquency involving a violent felony.

(f)

In the case of a person who knowingly violates section 922(p), such person shall be fined under this title, or imprisoned not more than 5 years, or both.

(g)

Whoever, with the intent to engage in conduct which -

(1)

constitutes an offense listed in section 1961(1),

(2)

is punishable under the Controlled Substances Act (21 U.S.C. 802 et seq.), the Controlled Substances Import and Export Act (21 U.S.C. 951 et seq.), or the Maritime Drug Law Enforcement Act (46 U.S.C. App. 1901 et seq.),

(3)

violates any State law relating to any controlled substance (as defined in section 102(6) of the Controlled Substances Act (21 U.S.C. 802(6))), or

(4)

constitutes a crime of violence (as defined in subsection (c)(3)), travels from any State or foreign country into any other State and acquires, transfers, or attempts to acquire or transfer, a firearm in such other State in furtherance of such purpose, shall be imprisoned not more than 10 years, fined in accordance with this title, or both.

(h)

Whoever knowingly transfers a firearm, knowing that such firearm will be used to commit a crime of violence (as defined in subsection (c)(3)) or drug trafficking crime (as defined in subsection (c)(2)) shall be imprisoned not more than 10 years, fined in accordance with this title, or both.

(i)

(1)

A person who knowingly violates section 922(u) shall be fined under this title, imprisoned not more than 10 years, or both.

(2)

Nothing contained in this subsection shall be construed as indicating an intent on the part of Congress to occupy the field in which provisions of this subsection operate to the exclusion of State laws on the same subject matter, nor shall any provision of this subsection be construed as invalidating any provision of State law unless such provision is inconsistent with any of the purposes of this subsection.

(j)

A person who, in the course of a violation of subsection (c), causes the death of a person through the use of a firearm, shall -

(1)

if the killing is a murder (as defined in section 1111), be punished by death or by imprisonment for any term of years or for life; and

(2)

if the killing is manslaughter (as defined in section 1112), be punished as provided in that section.

(k)

A person who, with intent to engage in or to promote conduct that -

(1)

is punishable under the Controlled Substances Act (21 U.S.C. 801 et seq.), the Controlled Substances Import and Export Act (21 U.S.C. 951 et seq.), or the Maritime Drug Law Enforcement Act (46 U.S.C. App. 1901 et seq.);

(2)

violates any law of a State relating to any controlled substance (as defined in section 102 of the Controlled Substances Act, 21 U.S.C. 802); or

(3)

constitutes a crime of violence (as defined in subsection (c)(3)), smuggles or knowingly brings into the United States a firearm, or attempts to do so, shall be imprisoned not more than 10 years, fined under this title, or both.

(l)

A person who steals any firearm which is moving as, or is a part of, or which has moved in, interstate or foreign commerce shall be imprisoned for not more than 10 years, fined under this title, or both.

(m)

A person who steals any firearm from a licensed importer, licensed manufacturer, licensed dealer, or licensed collector shall be fined under this title, imprisoned not more than 10 years, or both.

(n)

A person who, with the intent to engage in conduct that constitutes a violation of section 922(a)(1)(A), travels from any State or foreign country into any other State and acquires, or attempts to acquire, a firearm in such other State in furtherance of such purpose shall be imprisoned for not more than 10 years.

(o)

A person who conspires to commit an offense under subsection (c) shall be imprisoned for not more than 20 years, fined under this title, or both; and if the firearm is a machinegun or destructive device, or is equipped with a firearm silencer or muffler, shall be imprisoned for any term of years or life

Prev | Next

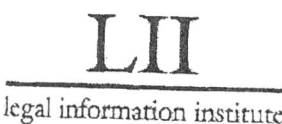

US CODE COLLECTION

search

TITLE 18 > PART I > CHAPTER 44 > Sec. 930.

Prev

Search this title:

Search Title 18

Notes
Updates
Parallel authorities
(CFR)
Topical references

Sec. 930. - Possession of firearms and dangerous weapons in Federal facilities

(a)

Except as provided in subsection (d), whoever knowingly possesses or causes to be present a firearm or other dangerous weapon in a Federal facility (other than a Federal court facility), or attempts to do so, shall be fined under this title or imprisoned not more than 1 year, or both.

(b)

Whoever, with intent that a firearm or other dangerous weapon be used in the commission of a crime, knowingly possesses or causes to be present such firearm or dangerous weapon in a Federal facility, or attempts to do so, shall be fined under this title or imprisoned not more than 5 years, or both.

(c)

A person who kills any person in the course of a violation of subsection (a) or (b), or in the course of an attack on a Federal facility involving the use of a firearm or other dangerous weapon, or attempts or conspires to do such an act, shall be punished as provided in sections 1111, 1112, 1113, and 1117.

(d)

Subsection (a) shall not apply to -

(1)

the lawful performance of official duties by an officer, agent, or employee of the United States, a State, or a political subdivision thereof, who is authorized by law to engage in or supervise the prevention, detection, investigation, or prosecution of any violation of law;

(2)

the possession of a firearm or other dangerous weapon by a Federal official or a member of the Armed Forces if such possession is authorized by law; or

(3)

the lawful carrying of firearms or other dangerous weapons in a Federal facility incident to hunting or other lawful purposes.

(e)

(1)

Except as provided in paragraph (2), whoever knowingly possesses or causes to be present a firearm in a Federal court facility, or attempts to do so, shall be fined under this title, imprisoned not more than 2 years, or both.

(2)

Paragraph (1) shall not apply to conduct which is described in paragraph (1) or (2) of subsection (d).

(f)

Nothing in this section limits the power of a court of the United States to punish for contempt or to promulgate rules or orders regulating, restricting, or prohibiting the possession of weapons within any building housing such court or any of its proceedings, or upon any grounds appurtenant to such building.

(9)

As used in this section:

(1)

The term "Federal facility" means a building or part thereof owned or leased by the Federal Government, where Federal employees are regularly present for the purpose of performing their official duties.

(2)

The term "dangerous weapon" means a weapon, device, instrument, material, or substance, animate or inanimate, that is used for, or is readily capable of, causing death or serious bodily injury, except that such term does not include a pocket knife with a blade of less than 2 1/2 inches in length.

(3)

The term "Federal court facility" means the courtroom, judges' chambers, witness rooms, jury deliberation rooms, attorney conference rooms, prisoner holding cells, offices of the court clerks, the United States attorney, and the United States marshal, probation and parole offices, and adjoining corridors of any court of the United States.

(h)

Notice of the provisions of subsections (a) and (b) shall be posted conspicuously at each public entrance to each Federal facility, and notice of subsection (e) shall be posted conspicuously at each public entrance to each Federal court facility, and no person shall be convicted of an offense under subsection (a) or (e) with respect to a Federal facility if such notice is not so posted at such facility, unless such person had actual notice of subsection (a) or (e), as the case may be

Prev

US CODE COLLECTION

search

TITLE 18 > PART I > CHAPTER 51 > Sec. 1111.

Next

Sec. 1111. - Murder

(a)

Murder is the unlawful killing of a human being with malice aforethought. Every murder perpetrated by poison, lying in wait, or any other kind of willful, deliberate, malicious, and premeditated killing; or committed in the perpetration of, or attempt to perpetrate, any arson, escape, murder, kidnapping, treason, espionage, sabotage, aggravated sexual abuse or sexual abuse, burglary, or robbery; or perpetrated from a premeditated design unlawfully and maliciously to effect the death of any human being other than him who is killed, is murder in the first degree. Any other murder is murder in the second degree.

(b)

Within the special maritime and territorial jurisdiction of the United States,

Whoever is guilty of murder in the first degree shall be punished by death or by imprisonment for life;

Whoever is guilty of murder in the second degree, shall be imprisoned for any term of years or for life

Search this title:

Search Title 18

Notes
Updates
Parallel authorities
(CFR)
Topical references

Next

US CODE COLLECTION

TITLE 18 > PART I > CHAPTER 51 > Sec. 1112.

Prev | Next

Sec. 1112. - Manslaughter

(a)

Manslaughter is the unlawful killing of a human being without malice. It is of two kinds: Voluntary - Upon a sudden quarrel or heat of passion. Involuntary - In the commission of an unlawful act not amounting to a felony, or in the commission in an unlawful manner, or without due caution and circumspection, of a lawful act which might produce death.

(b)

Within the special maritime and territorial jurisdiction of the United States,

Whoever is guilty of voluntary manslaughter, shall be fined under this title or imprisoned not more than ten years, or both;

Whoever is guilty of involuntary manslaughter, shall be fined under this title or imprisoned not more than six years, or both

Search this title:

Search Title 18

Notes
Updates
Parallel authorities (CFR)
Topical references

Prev | Next

legal information institute

collection home

US CODE COLLECTION

search

TITLE 18 > **PART I** > **CHAPTER 51** > **Sec. 1113.**

Prev | Next

Sec. 1113. - Attempt to commit murder or manslaughter

Except as provided in section 113 of this title, whoever, within the special maritime and territorial jurisdiction of the United States, attempts to commit murder or manslaughter, shall, for an attempt to commit murder be imprisoned not more than twenty years or fined under this title, or both, and for an attempt to commit manslaughter be imprisoned not more than seven years or fined under this title, or both

Search this title:

Search Title 18

Notes
Updates
Parallel authorities
(CFR)
Topical references

Prev | Next

about us

send email

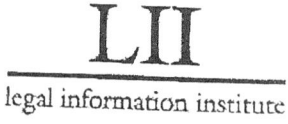

US CODE COLLECTION

TITLE 18 > **PART I** > **CHAPTER 51** > **Sec. 1114.**

Prev | Next

Sec. 1114. - Protection of officers and employees of the United States

Whoever kills or attempts to kill any officer or employee of the United States or of any agency in any branch of the United States Government (including any member of the uniformed services) while such officer or employee is engaged in or on account of the performance of official duties, or any person assisting such an officer or employee in the performance of such duties or on account of that assistance, shall be punished -

(1)

in the case of murder, as provided under section 1111;

(2)

in the case of manslaughter, as provided under section 1112; or

(3)

in the case of attempted murder or manslaughter, as provided in section 1113

Search this title:

Search Title 18

Notes
Updates
Parallel authorities
(CFR)
Topical references

Prev | Next

US CODE COLLECTION

Prev | Next

Search this title:

Search Title 18

Notes
Updates
Parallel authorities
(CFR)
Topical references

Sec. 1116. - Murder or manslaughter of foreign officials, official guests, or internationally protected persons

(a)

Whoever kills or attempts to kill a foreign official, official guest, or internationally protected person shall be punished as provided under sections 1111, 1112, and 1113 of this title.

(b)

For the purposes of this section:

(1)

"Family" includes

(a)

a spouse, parent, brother or sister, child, or person to whom the foreign official or internationally protected person stands in loco parentis, or

(b)

any other person living in his household and related to the foreign official or internationally protected person by blood or marriage.

(2)

"Foreign government" means the government of a foreign country, irrespective of recognition by the United States.

(3)

"Foreign official" means -

(A)

a Chief of State or the political equivalent, President, Vice President, Prime Minister, Ambassador, Foreign Minister, or other officer of Cabinet rank or above of a foreign government or the chief executive officer of an international organization, or any person who has previously served in such capacity, and any member of his family, while in the United States; and

(B)

any person of a foreign nationality who is duly notified to the United States as an officer or employee of a foreign government or international organization, and who is in the United States on official business, and any member of his family whose presence in the United States is in connection with the presence of such officer or employee.

(4)

"Internationally protected person" means -

(A)

a Chief of State or the political equivalent, head of government, or Foreign Minister whenever such person is in a country other than his own and any member of his family accompanying him; or

(B)

any other representative, officer, employee, or agent of the United States Government, a foreign government, or international organization who at the time and place concerned is entitled pursuant to international law to special protection against attack upon his person, freedom, or dignity, and any member of his family then forming part of his household.

(5)

"International organization" means a public international organization designated as such pursuant to section 1 of the International Organizations Immunities Act (22 U.S.C. 288) or a public organization created pursuant to treaty or other agreement under international law as an instrument through or by which two or more foreign governments engage in some aspect of their conduct of international affairs.

(6)

"Official guest" means a citizen or national of a foreign country present in the United States as an official guest of the Government of the United States pursuant to designation as such by the Secretary of State.

(7)

"National of the United States" has the meaning prescribed in section 101(a)(22) of the Immigration and Nationality Act (8 U.S.C. 1101(a)(22)).

(c)

If the victim of an offense under subsection (a) is an internationally protected person outside the United States, the United States may exercise jurisdiction over the offense if

(1)

the victim is a representative, officer, employee, or agent of the United States,

(2)

an offender is a national of the United States, or

(3)

an offender is afterwards found in the United States. As used in this subsection, the United States includes all areas under the jurisdiction of the United States including any of the places within the provisions of sections 5 and 7 of this title and section 46501(2) of title 49.

(d)

In the course of enforcement of this section and any other sections prohibiting a conspiracy or attempt to violate this section, the Attorney General may request assistance from any Federal, State, or local agency, including the Army, Navy, and Air Force, any statute, rule, or regulation to the contrary notwithstanding

Prev | Next

legal information institute

collection home

US CODE COLLECTION

search

TITLE 18 > PART I > CHAPTER 51 > Sec. 1118.

Prev | Next

Sec. 1118. - Murder by a Federal prisoner

(a) Offense. -

A person who, while confined in a Federal correctional institution under a sentence for a term of life imprisonment, commits the murder of another shall be punished by death or by life imprisonment.

(b) Definitions. -

In this section -

"Federal correctional institution" means any Federal prison, Federal correctional facility, Federal community program center, or Federal halfway house. "murder" means a first degree or second degree murder (as defined in section 1111). "term of life imprisonment" means a sentence for the term of natural life, a sentence commuted to natural life, an indeterminate term of a minimum of at least fifteen years and a maximum of life, or an unexecuted sentence of death

Search this title:

Search Title 18

Notes
Updates
Parallel authorities
(CFR)
Topical references

Prev | Next

 **US CODE COLLECTION**

collection home

search

TITLE 18 > PART I > CHAPTER 51 > Sec. 1119.

Prev | Next

Sec. 1119. - Foreign murder of United States nationals

(a) Definition. -

In this section, "national of the United States" has the meaning stated in section 101(a)(22) of the Immigration and Nationality Act (8 U.S.C. 1101(a)(22)).

(b) Offense. -

A person who, being a national of the United States, kills or attempts to kill a national of the United States while such national is outside the United States but within the jurisdiction of another country shall be punished as provided under sections 1111, 1112, and 1113.

(c) Limitations on Prosecution. -

(1)

No prosecution may be instituted against any person under this section except upon the written approval of the Attorney General, the Deputy Attorney General, or an Assistant Attorney General, which function of approving prosecutions may not be delegated. No prosecution shall be approved if prosecution has been previously undertaken by a foreign country for the same conduct.

(2)

No prosecution shall be approved under this section unless the Attorney General, in consultation with the Secretary of State, determines that the conduct took place in a country in which the person is no longer present, and the country lacks the ability to lawfully secure the person's return. A determination by the Attorney General under this paragraph is not subject to judicial review

Search this title:

Search Title 18

Notes
Updates
Parallel authorities
(CFR)
Topical references

US CODE COLLECTION

collection home

TITLE 18 > PART I > CHAPTER 51 > Sec. 1120.　　　　　Prev | Next

Sec. 1120. - Murder by escaped prisoners

(a) Definition. -

In this section, "Federal correctional institution" and "term of life imprisonment" have the meanings stated in section 1118.

(b) Offense and Penalty. -

A person, having escaped from a Federal correctional institution where the person was confined under a sentence for a term of life imprisonment, kills another shall be punished as provided in sections 1111 and 1112.

Search this title:

Search Title 18

Notes
Updates
Parallel authorities
(CFR)
Topical references

Prev | Next

© copyright　　　　about us　　　　send email

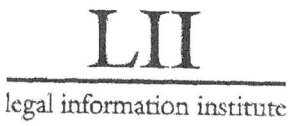

US CODE COLLECTION

search

TITLE 18 > PART I > CHAPTER 51 > Sec. 1121.

Prev | Next

Sec. 1121. - Killing persons aiding Federal investigations or State correctional officers

Search this title:

Search Title 18

Notes
Updates
Parallel authorities
(CFR)
Topical references

(a)

Whoever intentionally kills -

(1)

a State or local official, law enforcement officer, or other officer or employee while working with Federal law enforcement officials in furtherance of a Federal criminal investigation -

(A)

while the victim is engaged in the performance of official duties;

(B)

because of the performance of the victim's official duties; or

(C)

because of the victim's status as a public servant; or

(2)

any person assisting a Federal criminal investigation, while that assistance is being rendered and because of it,

shall be sentenced according to the terms of section 1111, including by sentence of death or by imprisonment for life.

(b)

(1)

Whoever, in a circumstance described in paragraph

(3) of this subsection, while incarcerated, intentionally kills any State correctional officer engaged in, or on account of the performance of such officer's official duties, shall be sentenced to a term of imprisonment which shall not be less than 20 years, and may be sentenced to life imprisonment or death.

(2)

As used in this section, the term, "State correctional officer" includes any officer or employee of any prison, jail, or other detention facility, operated by, or under contract to, either a State or local governmental agency, whose job responsibilities include providing for the custody of incarcerated individuals.

(3)

The circumstance referred to in paragraph (1) is that -

(A)

the correctional officer is engaged in transporting the incarcerated person interstate; or

(B)

the incarcerated person is incarcerated pursuant to a conviction for an offense against the United States.

(c)

For the purposes of this section, the term "State" means a State of the United States, the District of Columbia, and any commonwealth, territory, or possession of the United States

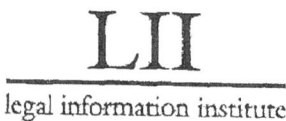

US CODE COLLECTION

search

Prev | Next

Sec. 1153. - Offenses committed within Indian country

Search this title:

(a)

Any Indian who commits against the person or property of another Indian or other person any of the following offenses, namely, murder, manslaughter, kidnapping, maiming, a felony under chapter 109A, incest, assault with intent to commit murder, assault with a dangerous weapon, assault resulting in serious bodily injury (as defined in section 1365 of this title), an assault against an individual who has not attained the age of 16 years, arson, burglary, robbery, and a felony under section 661 of this title within the Indian country, shall be subject to the same law and penalties as all other persons committing any of the above offenses, within the exclusive jurisdiction of the United States.

(b)

Any offense referred to in subsection (a) of this section that is not defined and punished by Federal law in force within the exclusive jurisdiction of the United States shall be defined and punished in accordance with the laws of the State in which such offense was committed as are in force at the time of such offense

Search Title 18

Notes
Updates
Parallel authorities
(CFR)
Topical references

Prev | Next

US CODE COLLECTION

search

Next

Search this title:

Search Title 18

Notes
Updates
Parallel authorities
(CFR)
Topical references

Sec. 1201. - Kidnapping

(a)

Whoever unlawfully seizes, confines, inveigles, decoys, kidnaps, abducts, or carries away and holds for ransom or reward or otherwise any person, except in the case of a minor by the parent thereof, when -

(1)

the person is willfully transported in interstate or foreign commerce, regardless of whether the person was alive when transported across a State boundary if the person was alive when the transportation began;

(2)

any such act against the person is done within the special maritime and territorial jurisdiction of the United States;

(3)

any such act against the person is done within the special aircraft jurisdiction of the United States as defined in section 46501 of title 49;

(4)

the person is a foreign official, an internationally protected person, or an official guest as those terms are defined in section 1116(b) of this title; or

(5)

the person is among those officers and employees described in section 1114 of this title and any such act against the person is done while the person is engaged in, or on account of, the performance of official duties,

shall be punished by imprisonment for any term of years

or for life and, if the death of any person results, shall be punished by death or life imprisonment.

(b)

With respect to subsection (a)(1), above, the failure to release the victim within twenty-four hours after he shall have been unlawfully seized, confined, inveigled, decoyed, kidnapped, abducted, or carried away shall create a rebuttable presumption that such person has been transported to interstate or foreign commerce. Notwithstanding the preceding sentence, the fact that the presumption under this section has not yet taken effect does not preclude a Federal investigation of a possible violation of this section before the 24-hour period has ended.

(c)

If two or more persons conspire to violate this section and one or more of such persons do any overt act to effect the object of the conspiracy, each shall be punished by imprisonment for any term of years or for life.

(d)

Whoever attempts to violate subsection (a) shall be punished by imprisonment for not more than twenty years.

(e)

If the victim of an offense under subsection (a) is an internationally protected person outside the United States, the United States may exercise jurisdiction over the offense if

(1)

the victim is a representative, officer, employee, or agent of the United States,

(2)

an offender is a national of the United States, or

(3)

an offender is afterwards found in the United States. As used in this subsection, the United States includes all areas under the jurisdiction of the United States including any of the places within the provisions of sections 5 and 7 of this title and section 46501(2) of title 49. For purposes of this subsection, the term "national of the United States" has the meaning prescribed in section 101(a)(22) of the Immigration and Nationality Act (8 U.S.C. 1101(a)

(22)).

(f)

In the course of enforcement of subsection (a)(4) and any other sections prohibiting a conspiracy or attempt to violate subsection (a)(4), the Attorney General may request assistance from any Federal, State, or local agency, including the Army, Navy, and Air Force, any statute, rule, or regulation to the contrary notwithstanding.

(g) Special Rule for Certain Offenses Involving Children. -

(1) To whom applicable. -

If -

(A)

the victim of an offense under this section has not attained the age of eighteen years; and

(B)

the offender -

(i)

has attained such age; and

(ii)

is not -

(I)

a parent;

(II)

a grandparent;

(III)

a brother;

(IV)

a sister;

(V)

an aunt;

(VI)

an uncle; or

(VII)

an individual having legal custody of the victim; the sentence under this section for such offense shall be subject to paragraph (2) of this subsection.

(2) Guidelines. -

The United States Sentencing Commission is directed to amend the existing guidelines for the offense of "kidnapping, abduction, or unlawful restraint," by including the following additional specific offense characteristics: If the victim was intentionally maltreated (i.e., denied either food or medical care) to a life-threatening degree, increase by 4 levels; if the victim was sexually exploited (i.e., abused, used involuntarily for pornographic purposes) increase by 3 levels; if the victim was placed in the care or custody of another person who does not have a legal right to such care or custody of the child either in exchange for money or other consideration, increase by 3 levels; if the defendant allowed the child to be subjected to any of the conduct specified in this section by another person, then increase by 2 levels.

(h)

As used in this section, the term "parent" does not include a person whose parental rights with respect to the victim of an offense under this section have been terminated by a final court order

Next

 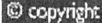

US CODE COLLECTION

Search this title:

Search Title 18

Sec. 1203. - Hostage taking

(a)

Except as provided in subsection (b) of this section, whoever, whether inside or outside the United States, seizes or detains and threatens to kill, to injure, or to continue to detain another person in order to compel a third person or a governmental organization to do or abstain from doing any act as an explicit or implicit condition for the release of the person detained, or attempts or conspires to do so, shall be punished by imprisonment for any term of years or for life and, if the death of any person results, shall be punished by death or life imprisonment.

(b)

(1)

It is not an offense under this section if the conduct required for the offense occurred outside the United States unless -

(A)

the offender or the person seized or detained is a national of the United States;

(B)

the offender is found in the United States; or

(C)

the governmental organization sought to be compelled is the Government of the United States.

(2)

It is not an offense under this section if the conduct required for the offense occurred inside the United States, each alleged offender and each person seized or detained are nationals of the United States, and each alleged offender is found in the United States, unless the governmental organization sought to be compelled is the Government of the United States.

(c)

As used in this section, the term "national of the United States" has the meaning given such term in section 101(a)(22) of the Immigration and Nationality Act (8 U.S.C. 1101 (a)(22))

Prev | Next

US CODE COLLECTION

search

Sec. 1365. - Tampering with consumer products

Search this title:

(a)

Whoever, with reckless disregard for the risk that another person will be placed in danger of death or bodily injury and under circumstances manifesting extreme indifference to such risk, tampers with any consumer product that affects interstate or foreign commerce, or the labeling of, or container for, any such product, or attempts to do so, shall -

Search Title 18

Notes
Updates
Parallel authorities
(CFR)
Topical references

(1)

in the case of an attempt, be fined under this title or imprisoned not more than ten years, or both;

(2)

if death of an individual results, be fined under this title or imprisoned for any term of years or for life, or both;

(3)

if serious bodily injury to any individual results, be fined under this title or imprisoned not more than twenty years, or both; and

(4)

in any other case, be fined under this title or imprisoned not more than ten years, or both.

(b)

Whoever, with intent to cause serious injury to the business of any person, taints any consumer product or renders materially false or misleading the labeling of, or container for, a consumer product, if such consumer product affects interstate or foreign commerce, shall be fined under this title or imprisoned not more than three years, or both.

(c)

(1)

Whoever knowingly communicates false information that a consumer product has been tainted, if such product or the results of such communication affect interstate or foreign commerce, and if such tainting, had it occurred, would create a risk of death or bodily injury to another person, shall be fined under this title or imprisoned not more than five years, or both.

(2)

As used in paragraph (1) of this subsection, the term "communicates false information" means communicates information that is false and that the communicator knows is false, under circumstances in which the information may reasonably be expected to be believed.

(d)

Whoever knowingly threatens, under circumstances in which the threat may reasonably be expected to be believed, that conduct that, if it occurred, would violate subsection (a) of this section will occur, shall be fined under this title or imprisoned not more than five years, or both.

(e)

Whoever is a party to a conspiracy of two or more persons to commit an offense under subsection (a) of this section, if any of the parties intentionally engages in any conduct in furtherance of such offense, shall be fined under this title or imprisoned not more than ten years, or both.

(f)

In addition to any other agency which has authority to investigate violations of this section, the Food and Drug Administration and the Department of Agriculture, respectively, have authority to investigate violations of this section involving a consumer product that is regulated by a provision of law such Administration or Department, as the case may be, administers.

(g)

As used in this section -

(1)

the term "consumer product" means -

(A)

any "food", "drug", "device", or "cosmetic", as those terms are respectively defined in section 201 of the Federal Food, Drug, and Cosmetic Act (21 U.S.C. 321); or

(B)

any article, product, or commodity which is customarily produced or distributed for consumption by individuals, or use by individuals for purposes of personal care or in the performance of services ordinarily rendered within the household, and which is designed to be consumed or expended in the course of such consumption or use;

(2)

the term "labeling" has the meaning given such term in section 201(m) of the Federal Food, Drug, and Cosmetic Act (21 U.S.C. 321(m));

(3)

the term "serious bodily injury" means bodily injury which involves -

(A)

a substantial risk of death;

(B)

extreme physical pain;

(C)

protracted and obvious disfigurement; or

(D)

protracted loss or impairment of the function of a bodily member, organ, or mental faculty; and

(4)

the term "bodily injury" means -

(A)

a cut, abrasion, bruise, burn, or disfigurement;

(B)

physical pain;

(C)

 illness;

(D)

 impairment of the function of a bodily member, organ, or mental faculty; or

(E)

 any other injury to the body, no matter how temporary

Prev | Next

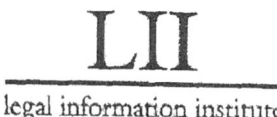

legal information institute

US CODE COLLECTION

collection home

search

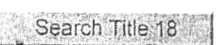

Next

Sec. 1501. - Assault on process server

Whoever knowingly and willfully obstructs, resists, or opposes any officer of the United States, or other person duly authorized, in serving, or attempting to serve or execute, any legal or judicial writ or process of any court of the United States, or United States magistrate judge; or

Whoever assaults, beats, or wounds any officer or other person duly authorized, knowing him to be such officer, or other person so duly authorized, in serving or executing any such writ, rule, order, process, warrant, or other legal or judicial writ or process -

Shall, except as otherwise provided by law, be fined under this title or imprisoned not more than one year, or both

Search this title:

Search Title 18

Notes
Updates
Parallel authorities
(CFR)
Topical references

Next

© copyright

about us

send email

US CODE COLLECTION

search

TITLE 18 > PART I > CHAPTER 73 > Sec. 1503.

Prev | Next

Search this title:

Search Title 18

Notes
Updates
Parallel authorities
(CFR)
Topical references

Sec. 1503. - Influencing or injuring officer or juror generally

(a)

Whoever corruptly, or by threats or force, or by any threatening letter or communication, endeavors to influence, intimidate, or impede any grand or petit juror, or officer in or of any court of the United States, or officer who may be serving at any examination or other proceeding before any United States magistrate judge or other committing magistrate, in the discharge of his duty, or injures any such grand or petit juror in his person or property on account of any verdict or indictment assented to by him, or on account of his being or having been such juror, or injures any such officer, magistrate judge, or other committing magistrate in his person or property on account of the performance of his official duties, or corruptly or by threats or force, or by any threatening letter or communication, influences, obstructs, or impedes, or endeavors to influence, obstruct, or impede, the due administration of justice, shall be punished as provided in subsection (b). If the offense under this section occurs in connection with a trial of a criminal case, and the act in violation of this section involves the threat of physical force or physical force, the maximum term of imprisonment which may be imposed for the offense shall be the higher of that otherwise provided by law or the maximum term that could have been imposed for any offense charged in such case.

(b)

The punishment for an offense under this section is -

(1)

in the case of a killing, the punishment provided in sections 1111 and 1112;

(2)

in the case of an attempted killing, or a case in which the offense was committed against a petit juror and in which a class A or B felony was charged, imprisonment for not more than 20 years, a fine under this title, or both; and

(3)

in any other case, imprisonment for not more than 10 years, a fine under this title, or both

US CODE COLLECTION

search

Prev | Next

Search this title:

Search Title 18

Notes
Updates
Parallel authorities
(CFR)
Topical references

Sec. 1505. - Obstruction of proceedings before departments, agencies, and committees

Whoever, with intent to avoid, evade, prevent, or obstruct compliance, in whole or in part, with any civil investigative demand duly and properly made under the Antitrust Civil Process Act, willfully withholds, misrepresents, removes from any place, conceals, covers up, destroys, mutilates, alters, or by other means falsifies any documentary material, answers to written interrogatories, or oral testimony, which is the subject of such demand; or attempts to do so or solicits another to do so; or

Whoever corruptly, or by threats or force, or by any threatening letter or communication influences, obstructs, or impedes or endeavors to influence, obstruct, or impede the due and proper administration of the law under which any pending proceeding is being had before any department or agency of the United States, or the due and proper exercise of the power of inquiry under which any inquiry or investigation is being had by either House, or any committee of either House or any joint committee of the Congress -

Shall be fined under this title or imprisoned not more than five years, or both

Prev | Next

US CODE COLLECTION

search

TITLE 18 > PART I > CHAPTER 73 > Sec. 1512.

Prev | Next

Search this title:

Search Title 18

Notes
Updates
Parallel authorities
(CFR)
Topical references

Sec. 1512. - Tampering with a witness, victim, or an informant

(a)

(1)

Whoever kills or attempts to kill another person, with intent to -

(A)

prevent the attendance or testimony of any person in an official proceeding;

(B)

prevent the production of a record, document, or other object, in an official proceeding; or

(C)

prevent the communication by any person to a law enforcement officer or judge of the United States of information relating to the commission or possible commission of a Federal offense or a violation of conditions of probation, parole, or release pending judicial proceedings;

shall be punished as provided in paragraph (2).

(2)

The punishment for an offense under this subsection is -

(A)

in the case of murder (as defined in section 1111), the death penalty or imprisonment for life, and in the case of any other killing, the punishment provided in section 1112; and

(B)

in the case of an attempt, imprisonment for not more than twenty years.

(b)

Whoever knowingly uses intimidation or physical force, threatens, or corruptly persuades another person, or attempts to do so, or engages in misleading conduct toward another person, with intent to -

(1)

influence, delay, or prevent the testimony of any person in an official proceeding;

(2)

cause or induce any person to -

(A)

withhold testimony, or withhold a record, document, or other object, from an official proceeding;

(B)

alter, destroy, mutilate, or conceal an object with intent to impair the object's integrity or availability for use in an official proceeding;

(C)

evade legal process summoning that person to appear as a witness, or to produce a record, document, or other object, in an official proceeding; or

(D)

be absent from an official proceeding to which such person has been summoned by legal process; or

(3)

hinder, delay, or prevent the communication to a law enforcement officer or judge of the United States of information relating to the commission or possible commission of a Federal offense or a violation of conditions of probation, parole, or release pending judicial proceedings;

shall be fined under this title or imprisoned not more than ten years, or both.

(c)

Whoever intentionally harasses another person and thereby hinders, delays, prevents, or dissuades any person from -

(1)

attending or testifying in an official proceeding;

(2)

reporting to a law enforcement officer or judge of the United States the commission or possible commission of a Federal offense or a violation of conditions of probation, parole, or release pending judicial proceedings;

(3)

arresting or seeking the arrest of another person in connection with a Federal offense; or

(4)

causing a criminal prosecution, or a parole or probation revocation proceeding, to be sought or instituted, or assisting in such prosecution or proceeding;

or attempts to do so, shall be fined under this title or imprisoned not more than one year, or both.

(d)

In a prosecution for an offense under this section, it is an affirmative defense, as to which the defendant has the burden of proof by a preponderance of the evidence, that the conduct consisted solely of lawful conduct and that the defendant's sole intention was to encourage, induce, or cause the other person to testify truthfully.

(e)

For the purposes of this section -

(1)

an official proceeding need not be pending or about to be instituted at the time of the offense; and

(2)

the testimony, or the record, document, or other object need not be admissible in evidence or free of a claim of privilege.

(f)

In a prosecution for an offense under this section, no state of mind need be proved with respect to the circumstance -

(1)

that the official proceeding before a judge, court, magistrate judge, grand jury, or government agency is before a judge or court of the United States, a United States magistrate judge, a bankruptcy judge, a Federal grand jury, or a Federal Government agency; or

(2)

that the judge is a judge of the United States or that the law enforcement officer is an officer or employee of the Federal Government or a person authorized to act for or on behalf of the Federal Government or serving the Federal Government as an adviser or consultant.

(g)

There is extraterritorial Federal jurisdiction over an offense under this section.

(h)

A prosecution under this section or section 1503 may be brought in the district in which the official proceeding (whether or not pending or about to be instituted) was intended to be affected or in the district in which the conduct constituting the alleged offense occurred.

(i)

If the offense under this section occurs in connection with a trial of a criminal case, the maximum term of imprisonment which may be imposed for the offense shall be the higher of that otherwise provided by law or the maximum term that could have been imposed for any offense charged in such case

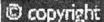

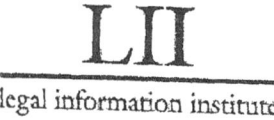

US CODE COLLECTION

search

TITLE 18 > PART I > CHAPTER 73 > Sec. 1513.

Prev | Next

Search this title:

Search Title 18

Notes
Updates
Parallel authorities
(CFR)
Topical references

Sec. 1513. - Retaliating against a witness, victim, or an informant

(a)

(1)

Whoever kills or attempts to kill another person with intent to retaliate against any person for -

(A)

the attendance of a witness or party at an official proceeding, or any testimony given or any record, document, or other object produced by a witness in an official proceeding; or

(B)

providing to a law enforcement officer any information relating to the commission or possible commission of a Federal offense or a violation of conditions of probation, parole, or release pending judicial proceedings,

shall be punished as provided in paragraph (2).

(2)

The punishment for an offense under this subsection is -

(A)

in the case of a killing, the punishment provided in sections 1111 and 1112; and

(B)

in the case of an attempt, imprisonment for not more than 20 years.

(b)

Whoever knowingly engages in any conduct and thereby causes bodily injury to another person or damages the tangible property of another person, or threatens to do so, with intent to retaliate against any person for -

(1)

the attendance of a witness or party at an official proceeding, or any testimony given or any record, document, or other object produced by a witness in an official proceeding; or

(2)

any information relating to the commission or possible commission of a Federal offense or a violation of conditions of probation, parole, or release pending judicial proceedings given by a person to a law enforcement officer;

or attempts to do so, shall be fined under this title or imprisoned not more than ten years, or both.

(c)

If the retaliation occurred because of attendance at or testimony in a criminal case, the maximum term of imprisonment which may be imposed for the offense under this section shall be the higher of that otherwise provided by law or the maximum term that could have been imposed for any offense charged in such case.

(d)

There is extraterritorial Federal jurisdiction over an offense under this section

Prev | Next

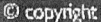

US CODE COLLECTION

search

Next

Search this title:

Search Title 18

Notes
Updates
Parallel authorities
(CFR)
Topical references

Sec. 1751. - Presidential and Presidential staff assassination, kidnapping, and assault; penalties

(a)

Whoever kills

(1)

any individual who is the President of the United States, the President-elect, the Vice President, or, if there is no Vice President, the officer next in the order of succession to the Office of the President of the United States, the Vice President-elect, or any person who is acting as President under the Constitution and laws of the United States, or

(2)

any person appointed under section 105(a)(2)(A) of title 3 employed in the Executive Office of the President or appointed under section 106(a)(1)(A) of title 3 employed in the Office of the Vice President, shall be punished as provided by sections 1111 and 1112 of this title.

(b)

Whoever kidnaps any individual designated in subsection (a) of this section shall be punished

(1)

by imprisonment for any term of years or for life, or

(2)

by death or imprisonment for any term of years or for life, if death results to such individual.

(c)

Whoever attempts to kill or kidnap any individual designated in subsection (a) of this section shall be punished by imprisonment for any term of years or for life.

(d)

If two or more persons conspire to kill or kidnap any individual designated in subsection (a) of this section and one or more of such persons do any act to effect the object of the conspiracy, each shall be punished

(1)

by imprisonment for any term of years or for life, or

(2)

by death or imprisonment for any term of years or for life, if death results to such individual.

(e)

Whoever assaults any person designated in subsection (a)(1) shall be fined under this title, or imprisoned not more than ten years, or both. Whoever assaults any person designated in subsection (a)(2) shall be fined under this title, or imprisoned not more than one year, or both; and if the assault involved the use of a dangerous weapon, or personal injury results, shall be fined under this title, or imprisoned not more than ten years, or both.

(f)

The terms "President-elect" and "Vice-President-elect" as used in this section shall mean such persons as are the apparent successful candidates for the offices of President and Vice President, respectively, as ascertained from the results of the general elections held to determine the electors of President and Vice President in accordance with title 3, United States Code, sections 1 and 2.

(g)

The Attorney General of the United States, in his discretion is authorized to pay an amount not to exceed $100,000 for information and services concerning a violation of subsection (a)(1). Any officer or employee of the United States or of any State or local government who furnishes information or renders service in the performance of his official duties shall not be eligible for payment under this subsection.

(h)

    If Federal investigative or prosecutive jurisdiction is asserted for a violation of this section, such assertion shall suspend the exercise of jurisdiction by a State or local authority, under any applicable State or local law, until Federal action is terminated.

(i)

    Violations of this section shall be investigated by the Federal Bureau of Investigation. Assistance may be requested from any Federal, State, or local agency, including the Army, Navy, and Air Force, any statute, rule, or regulation to the contrary notwithstanding.

(j)

    In a prosecution for an offense under this section the Government need not prove that the defendant knew that the victim of the offense was an official protected by this section.

(k)

    There is extraterritorial jurisdiction over the conduct prohibited by this section

Next

US CODE COLLECTION

Search this title:

Search Title 18

Notes
Updates
Parallel authorities
(CFR)
Topical references

Sec. 1864. - Hazardous or injurious devices on Federal lands

(a)

Whoever -

(1)

with the intent to violate the Controlled Substances Act,

(2)

with the intent to obstruct or harass the harvesting of timber, or

(3)

with reckless disregard to the risk that another person will be placed in danger of death or bodily injury and under circumstances manifesting extreme indifference to such risk,

uses a hazardous or injurious device on Federal land, on an Indian reservation, or on an Indian allotment while the title to such allotment is held in trust by the United States or while such allotment remains inalienable by the allottee without the consent of the United States shall be punished under subsection (b).

(b)

An individual who violates subsection (a) shall -

(1)

if death of an individual results, be fined under this title or imprisoned for any term of years or for life, or both;

(2)

if serious bodily injury to any individual results, be fined under this title or imprisoned for not more than 40 years, or both;

(3)

if bodily injury to any individual results, be fined under this title or imprisoned for not more than 20 years, or both;

(4)

if damage to the property of any individual results or if avoidance costs have been incurred exceeding $10,000, in the aggregate, be fined under this title or imprisoned for not more than 20 years, or both; and

(5)

in any other case, be fined under this title or imprisoned for not more than one year.

(c)

Any individual who is punished under subsection (b)(5) after one or more prior convictions under any such subsection shall be fined under this title or imprisoned for not more than 20 years, or both.

(d)

As used in this section -

(1)

the term "serious bodily injury" means bodily injury which involves -

(A)

a substantial risk of death;

(B)

extreme physical pain;

(C)

protracted and obvious disfigurement; and

(D)

protracted loss or impairment of the function of bodily member, organ, or mental faculty;

(2)

the term "bodily injury" means -

(A)

a cut, abrasion, bruise, burn, or disfigurement;

(B)

physical pain;

(C)

illness;

(D)

impairment of the function of a bodily member, organ, or mental faculty; or

(E)

any other injury to the body, no matter how temporary;

(3)

the term "hazardous or injurious device" means a device, which when assembled or placed, is capable of causing bodily injury, or damage to property, by the action of any person making contact with such device subsequent to the assembly or placement. Such term includes guns attached to trip wires or other triggering mechanisms, ammunition attached to trip wires or other triggering mechanisms, or explosive devices attached to trip wires or other triggering mechanisms, sharpened stakes, lines or wires, lines or wires with hooks attached, nails placed so that the sharpened ends are positioned in an upright manner, or tree spiking devices including spikes, nails, or other objects hammered, driven, fastened, or otherwise placed into or on any timber, whether or not severed from the stump; and

(4)

the term "avoidance costs" means costs incurred by any individual for the purpose of -

(A)

detecting a hazardous or injurious device; or

(B)

preventing death, serious bodily injury, bodily injury, or property damage likely to result from the use of a hazardous or injurious device in violation of subsection (a).

(e)

Any person injured as the result of a violation of subsection (a) may commence a civil action on his own behalf against any person who is alleged to be in violation of subsection (a). The district courts shall have jurisdiction, without regard to the amount in controversy or the citizenship of the parties, in such civil actions. The court may award, in addition to monetary damages for any injury resulting from an alleged violation of subsection (a), costs of litigation, including reasonable attorney and expert witness fees, to any prevailing or substantially prevailing party, whenever the court determines such award is appropriate

Prev

US CODE COLLECTION

search

<u>TITLE 18</u> > PART I > <u>CHAPTER</u> 95 > Sec. 1951.

Next

Search this title:

Search Title 18

Notes
Updates
Parallel authorities
(CFR)
Topical references

Sec. 1951. - Interference with commerce by threats or violence

(a)

Whoever in any way or degree obstructs, delays, or affects commerce or the movement of any article or commodity in commerce, by robbery or extortion or attempts or conspires so to do, or commits or threatens physical violence to any person or property in furtherance of a plan or purpose to do anything in violation of this section shall be fined under this title or imprisoned not more than twenty years, or both.

(b)

As used in this section -

(1)

The term ''robbery'' means the unlawful taking or obtaining of personal property from the person or in the presence of another, against his will, by means of actual or threatened force, or violence, or fear of injury, immediate or future, to his person or property, or property in his custody or possession, or the person or property of a relative or member of his family or of anyone in his company at the time of the taking or obtaining.

(2)

The term ''extortion'' means the obtaining of property from another, with his consent, induced by wrongful use of actual or threatened force, violence, or fear, or under color of official right.

(3)

The term ''commerce'' means commerce within the District of Columbia, or any Territory or Possession of the

United States; all commerce between any point in a State, Territory, Possession, or the District of Columbia and any point outside thereof; all commerce between points within the same State through any place outside such State; and all other commerce over which the United States has jurisdiction.

(c)

This section shall not be construed to repeal, modify or affect section 17 of Title 15, sections 52, 101-115, 151-166 of Title 29 or sections 151-188 of Title 45

Next

US CODE COLLECTION

search

TITLE 18 > PART I > CHAPTER 95 > Sec. 1952.

Prev | Next

Search this title:

[   ]

Search Title 18

Notes
Updates
Parallel authorities
(CFR)
Topical references

Sec. 1952. - Interstate and foreign travel or transportation in aid of racketeering enterprises

(a)

Whoever travels in interstate or foreign commerce or uses the mail or any facility in interstate or foreign commerce, with intent to -

(1)

distribute the proceeds of any unlawful activity; or

(2)

commit any crime of violence to further any unlawful activity; or

(3)

otherwise promote, manage, establish, carry on, or facilitate the promotion, management, establishment, or carrying on, of any unlawful activity,

and thereafter performs or attempts to perform -

(A)

an act described in paragraph (1) or (3) shall be fined under this title, imprisoned not more than 5 years, or both; or

(B)

an act described in paragraph (2) shall be fined under this title, imprisoned for not more than 20 years, or both, and if death results shall be imprisoned for any term of years or for life.

(b)

As used in this section (i) "unlawful activity" means

(1)

any business enterprise involving gambling, liquor on which the Federal excise tax has not been paid, narcotics or controlled substances (as defined in section 102(6) of the Controlled Substances Act), or prostitution offenses in violation of the laws of the State in which they are committed or of the United States,

(2)

extortion, bribery, or arson in violation of the laws of the State in which committed or of the United States, or

(3)

any act which is indictable under subchapter II of chapter 53 of title 31, United States Code, or under section 1956 or 1957 of this title and

(ii)

the term "State" includes a State of the United States, the District of Columbia, and any commonwealth, territory, or possession of the United States.

(c)

Investigations of violations under this section involving liquor shall be conducted under the supervision of the Secretary of the Treasury

Prev | Next

US CODE COLLECTION

search

Prev | Next

Search this title:

Search Title 18

Notes
Updates
Parallel authorities
(CFR)
Topical references

Sec. 1958. - Use of interstate commerce facilities in the commission of murder-for-hire

(a)

Whoever travels in or causes another (including the intended victim) to travel in interstate or foreign commerce, or uses or causes another (including the intended victim) to use the mail or any facility in interstate or foreign commerce, with intent that a murder be committed in violation of the laws of any State or the United States as consideration for the receipt of, or as consideration for a promise or agreement to pay, anything of pecuniary value, or who conspires to do so, shall be fined under this title or imprisoned for not more than ten years, or both; and if personal injury results, shall be fined under this title or imprisoned for not more than twenty years, or both; and if death results, shall be punished by death or life imprisonment, or shall be fined not more than $250,000, or both.

(b)

As used in this section and section 1959 -

(1)

"anything of pecuniary value" means anything of value in the form of money, a negotiable instrument, a commercial interest, or anything else the primary significance of which is economic advantage;

(2)

"facility of interstate commerce" includes means of transportation and communication; and

(3)

"State" includes a State of the United States, the District of Columbia, and any commonwealth, territory, or possession of the United States

about us

send email

US CODE COLLECTION

search

TITLE 18 > PART I > CHAPTER 95 > Sec. 1959.

Prev | Next

Search this title:

Search Title 18

Notes
Updates
Parallel authorities
(CFR)
Topical references

Sec. 1959. - Violent crimes in aid of racketeering activity

(a)

Whoever, as consideration for the receipt of, or as consideration for a promise or agreement to pay, anything of pecuniary value from an enterprise engaged in racketeering activity, or for the purpose of gaining entrance to or maintaining or increasing position in an enterprise engaged in racketeering activity, murders, kidnaps, maims, assaults with a dangerous weapon, commits assault resulting in serious bodily injury upon, or threatens to commit a crime of violence against any individual in violation of the laws of any State or the United States, or attempts or conspires so to do, shall be punished -

(1)

for murder, by death or life imprisonment, or a fine under this title, or both; and for kidnapping, by imprisonment for any term of years or for life, or a fine under this title, or both;

(2)

for maiming, by imprisonment for not more than thirty years or a fine under this title, or both;

(3)

for assault with a dangerous weapon or assault resulting in serious bodily injury, by imprisonment for not more than twenty years or a fine under this title, or both;

(4)

for threatening to commit a crime of violence, by imprisonment for not more than five years or a fine under this title, or both;

(5)

for attempting or conspiring to commit murder or kidnapping, by imprisonment for not more than ten years or a fine under this title, or both; and

(6)

for attempting or conspiring to commit a crime involving maiming, assault with a dangerous weapon, or assault resulting in serious bodily injury, by imprisonment for not more than three years or a fine of [1] under this title, or both.

(b)

As used in this section -

(1)

"racketeering activity" has the meaning set forth in section 1961 of this title; and

(2)

"enterprise" includes any partnership, corporation, association, or other legal entity, and any union or group of individuals associated in fact although not a legal entity, which is engaged in, or the activities of which affect, interstate or foreign commerce

---

[1] So in original. The word "of" probably should not appear.

Prev | Next

legal information institute

collection home

US CODE COLLECTION

search

Prev | Next

TITLE 18 > PART I > CHAPTER 103 > Sec. 2113.

Search this title:

Search Title 18

Notes
Updates
Parallel authorities
(CFR)
Topical references

Sec. 2113. - Bank robbery and incidental crimes

(a)

Whoever, by force and violence, or by intimidation, takes, or attempts to take, from the person or presence of another, or obtains or attempts to obtain by extortion any property or money or any other thing of value belonging to, or in the care, custody, control, management, or possession of, any bank, credit union, or any savings and loan association; or

Whoever enters or attempts to enter any bank, credit union, or any savings and loan association, or any building used in whole or in part as a bank, credit union, or as a savings and loan association, with intent to commit in such bank, credit union, or in such savings and loan association, or building, or part thereof, so used, any felony affecting such bank, credit union, or such savings and loan association and in violation of any statute of the

United States, or any larceny -

Shall be fined under this title or imprisoned not more than twenty years, or both.

(b)

Whoever takes and carries away, with intent to steal or purloin, any property or money or any other thing of value exceeding $1,000 belonging to, or in the care, custody, control, management, or possession of any bank, credit union, or any savings and loan association, shall be fined under this title or imprisoned not more than ten years, or both; or

Whoever takes and carries away, with intent to steal or purloin, any property or money or any other thing of value not exceeding $1,000 belonging to, or in the care, custody, control, management, or possession of any bank, credit union, or any savings and loan association, shall be fined not more than $1,000 or imprisoned not more than one year, or both.

(c)

Whoever receives, possesses, conceals, stores, barters, sells, or disposes of, any property or money or other thing of value which has been taken or stolen from a bank, credit union, or savings and loan association in violation of subsection (b), knowing the same to be property which has been stolen shall be subject to the punishment provided in subsection (b) for the taker.

(d)

Whoever, in committing, or in attempting to commit, any offense defined in subsections (a) and (b) of this section, assaults any person, or puts in jeopardy the life of any person by the use of a dangerous weapon or device, shall be fined under this title or imprisoned not more than twenty-five years, or both.

(e)

Whoever, in committing any offense defined in this section, or in avoiding or attempting to avoid apprehension for the commission of such offense, or in freeing himself or attempting to free himself from arrest or confinement for such offense, kills any person, or forces any person to accompany him without the consent of such person, shall be imprisoned not less than ten years, or if death results shall be punished by death or life imprisonment.

(f)

As used in this section the term "bank" means any member bank of the Federal Reserve System, and any bank, banking association, trust company, savings bank, or other banking institution organized or operating under the laws of the United States, including a branch or agency of a foreign bank (as such terms are defined in paragraphs (1) and (3) of section 1(b) of the International Banking Act of 1978), and any institution the deposits of which are insured by the Federal Deposit Insurance Corporation.

(g)

As used in this section the term "credit union" means any Federal credit union and any State-chartered credit union the accounts of which are insured by the National Credit Union Administration Board, and any "Federal credit union" as defined in section 2 of the Federal Credit Union Act. The term "State-chartered credit union" includes a credit union chartered under the laws of a State of the United States, the District of Columbia, or any commonwealth, territory, or possession of the United States.

(h)

As used in this section, the term "savings and loan association" means -

(1)

a Federal savings association or State savings association (as defined in section 3(b) of the Federal Deposit Insurance Act (12 U.S.C. 1813(b))) having accounts insured by the Federal Deposit Insurance Corporation; and

(2)

a corporation described in section 3(b)(1)(C) of the Federal Deposit Insurance Act (12 U.S.C. 1813(b)(1)(C)) that is operating under the laws of the United States

Prev | Next

US CODE COLLECTION

collection home

TITLE 18 > PART I > CHAPTER 103 > Sec. 2114.

Prev | Next

Sec. 2114. - Mail, money, or other property of United States

(a) Assault. -

A person who assaults any person having lawful charge, control, or custody of any mail matter or of any money or other property of the United States, with intent to rob, steal, or purloin such mail matter, money, or other property of the United States, or robs or attempts to rob any such person of mail matter, or of any money, or other property of the United States, shall, for the first offense, be imprisoned not more than ten years; and if in effecting or attempting to effect such robbery he wounds the person having custody of such mail, money, or other property of the United States, or puts his life in jeopardy by the use of a dangerous weapon, or for a subsequent offense, shall be imprisoned not more than twenty-five years.

(b) Receipt, Possession, Concealment, or Disposal of Property. -

A person who receives, possesses, conceals, or disposes of any money or other property that has been obtained in violation of this section, knowing the same to have been unlawfully obtained, shall be imprisoned not more than 10 years, fined under this title, or both.

Search this title:

Search Title 18

Notes
Updates
Parallel authorities (CFR)
Topical references

Prev | Next

legal information institute

US CODE COLLECTION

collection home

search

TITLE 18 > PART I > CHAPTER 103 > Sec. 2116.

Prev | Next

Search this title:

Search Title 18

Sec. 2116. - Railway or steamboat post office

Whoever, by violence, enters a post-office car, or any part of any car, steamboat, or vessel, assigned to the use of the mail service, or willfully or maliciously assaults or interferes with any postal clerk in the discharge of his duties in connection with such car, steamboat, vessel, or apartment thereof, shall be fined under this title or imprisoned not more than three years, or both

Notes
Updates
Parallel authorities (CFR)
Topical references

Prev | Next

US CODE COLLECTION

Search this title:

Search Title 18

Notes
Updates
Parallel authorities
(CFR)
Topical references

Sec. 2118. - Robberies and burglaries involving controlled substances

(a)

Whoever takes or attempts to take from the person or presence of another by force or violence or by intimidation any material or compound containing any quantity of a controlled substance belonging to or in the care, custody, control, or possession of a person registered with the Drug Enforcement Administration under section 302 of the Controlled Substances Act (21 U.S.C. 822) shall, except as provided in subsection (c), be fined under this title or imprisoned not more than twenty years, or both, if

(1)

the replacement cost of the material or compound to the registrant was not less than $500,

(2)

the person who engaged in such taking or attempted such taking traveled in interstate or foreign commerce or used any facility in interstate or foreign commerce to facilitate such taking or attempt, or

(3)

another person was killed or suffered significant bodily injury as a result of such taking or attempt.

(b)

Whoever, without authority, enters or attempts to enter, or remains in, the business premises or property of a person registered with the Drug Enforcement Administration under section 302 of the Controlled Substances Act (21 U.S.C. 822) with the intent to steal any material or compound containing any quantity of a controlled substance shall, except as provided in subsection (c), be fined under this title or imprisoned not more than twenty years, or both, if

(1)

the replacement cost of the controlled substance to the registrant was not less than $500,

(2)

the person who engaged in such entry or attempted such entry or who remained in such premises or property traveled in interstate or foreign commerce or used any facility in interstate or foreign commerce to facilitate such entry or attempt or to facilitate remaining in such premises or property, or

(3)

another person was killed or suffered significant bodily injury as a result of such entry or attempt.

(c)

(1)

Whoever in committing any offense under subsection (a) or (b) assaults any person, or puts in jeopardy the life of any person, by the use of a dangerous weapon or device shall be fined under this title and imprisoned for not more than twenty-five years.

(2)

Whoever in committing any offense under subsection (a) or (b) kills any person shall be fined under this title or imprisoned for any term of years or life, or both.

(d)

If two or more persons conspire to violate subsection (a) or (b) of this section and one or more of such persons do any overt act to effect the object of the conspiracy, each shall be fined under this title or imprisoned not more than ten years or both.

(e)

For purposes of this section -

(1)

the term "controlled substance" has the meaning prescribed for that term by section 102 of the Controlled Substances Act;

(2)

the term "business premises or property" includes conveyances and storage facilities; and

(3)

the term "significant bodily injury" means bodily injury which involves a risk of death, significant physical pain, protracted and obvious disfigurement, or a protracted loss or impairment of the function of a bodily member, organ, or mental or sensory faculty

Prev | Next

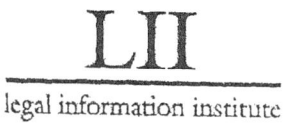

US CODE COLLECTION

Prev

Sec. 2119. - Motor vehicles

Whoever, with the intent to cause death or serious bodily harm shipped, or received in interstate or foreign commerce from the person or presence of another by force and violence or by intimidation, or attempts to do so, shall -

(1)

be fined under this title or imprisoned not more than 15 years, or both,

(2)

if serious bodily injury (as defined in section 1365 of this title, including any conduct that, if the conduct occurred in the special maritime and territorial jurisdiction of the United States, would violate section 2241 or 2242 of this title) results, be fined under this title or imprisoned not more than 25 years, or both, and

(3)

if death results, be fined under this title or imprisoned for any number of years up to life, or both, or sentenced to death

Search this title:

Search Title 18

Notes
Updates
Parallel authorities
(CFR)
Topical references

---

[1] takes a motor vehicle that has been transported,

[1] So in original. Probably should be followed by a comma.

Prev

US CODE COLLECTION

search

TITLE 18 > PART I > CHAPTER 107 > Sec. 2191.

Next

Sec. 2191. - Cruelty to seamen

Whoever, being the master or officer of a vessel of the United States, on the high seas, or on any other waters within the admiralty and maritime jurisdiction of the United States, flogs, beats, wounds, or without justifiable cause, imprisons any of the crew of such vessel, or withholds from them suitable food and nourishment, or inflicts upon them any corporal or other cruel and unusual punishment, shall be fined under this title or imprisoned not more than five years, or both

Search this title:

Search Title 18

Notes
Updates
Parallel authorities
(CFR)
Topical references

Next

© copyright   about us   send email

US CODE COLLECTION

search

TITLE 18 > PART I > CHAPTER 109 > Sec. 2231.

Next

Sec. 2231. - Assault or resistance

(a)

Whoever forcibly assaults, resists, opposes, prevents, impedes, intimidates, or interferes with any person authorized to serve or execute search warrants or to make searches and seizures while engaged in the performance of his duties with regard thereto or on account of the performance of such duties, shall be fined under this title or imprisoned not more than three years, or both; and -

(b)

Whoever, in committing any act in violation of this section, uses any deadly or dangerous weapon, shall be fined under this title or imprisoned not more than ten years, or both

Search this title:

Search Title 18

Notes
Updates
Parallel authorities
(CFR)
Topical references

Next

© copyright   about us   send email

US CODE COLLECTION

search

Next

Search this title:

Search Title 18

Notes
Updates
Parallel authorities
(CFR)
Topical references

Sec. 2241. - Aggravated sexual abuse

(a) By Force or Threat. -

Whoever, in the special maritime and territorial jurisdiction of the United States or in a Federal prison, knowingly causes another person to engage in a sexual act -

(1)

by using force against that other person; or

(2)

by threatening or placing that other person in fear that any person will be subjected to death, serious bodily injury, or kidnapping;

or attempts to do so, shall be fined under this title, imprisoned for any term of years or life, or both.

(b) By Other Means. -

Whoever, in the special maritime and territorial jurisdiction of the United States or in a Federal prison, knowingly -

(1)

renders another person unconscious and thereby engages in a sexual act with that other person; or

(2)

administers to another person by force or threat of force, or without the knowledge or permission of that person, a drug, intoxicant, or other similar substance and thereby -

(A)

substantially impairs the ability of that other person to appraise or control conduct; and

(B)

engages in a sexual act with that other person; or attempts to do so, shall be fined under this title, imprisoned for any term of years or life, or both.

(c) With Children. -

Whoever crosses a State line with intent to engage in a sexual act with a person who has not attained the age of 12 years, or in the special maritime and territorial jurisdiction of the United States or in a Federal prison, knowingly engages in a sexual act with another person who has not attained the age of 12 years, or knowingly engages in a sexual act under the circumstances described in subsections (a) and (b) with another person who has attained the age of 12 years but has not attained the age of 16 years (and is at least 4 years younger than the person so engaging), or attempts to do so, shall be fined under this title, imprisoned for any term of years or life, or both. If the defendant has previously been convicted of another Federal offense under this subsection, or of a State offense that would have been an offense under either such provision had the offense occurred in a Federal prison, unless the death penalty is imposed, the defendant shall be sentenced to life in prison.

(d) State of Mind Proof Requirement. -

In a prosecution under subsection (c) of this section, the Government need not prove that the defendant knew that the other person engaging in the sexual act had not attained the age of 12 years.

Next

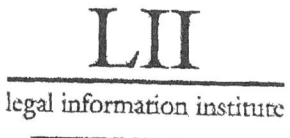

US CODE COLLECTION

Prev | Next

Search this title:

Search Title 18

Notes
Updates
Parallel authorities
(CFR)
Topical references

Sec. 2245. - Sexual abuse resulting in death

A person who, in the course of an offense under this chapter, engages in conduct that results in the death of a person, shall be punished by death or imprisoned for any term of years or for life

Prev | Next

© copyright   about us   send email

US CODE COLLECTION

TITLE 18 > PART I > CHAPTER 110A > Sec. 2261.

Next

Search this title:

[   ]

Search Title 18

Notes
Updates
Parallel authorities
(CFR)
Topical references

Sec. 2261. - Interstate domestic violence

(a) Offenses. -

(1) Travel or conduct of offender. -

A person who travels in interstate or foreign commerce or enters or leaves Indian country with the intent to kill, injure, harass, or intimidate a spouse or intimate partner, and who, in the course of or as a result of such travel, commits or attempts to commit a crime of violence against that spouse or intimate partner, shall be punished as provided in subsection (b).

(2) Causing travel of victim. -

A person who causes a spouse or intimate partner to travel in interstate or foreign commerce or to enter or leave Indian country by force, coercion, duress, or fraud, and who, in the course of, as a result of, or to facilitate such conduct or travel, commits or attempts to commit a crime of violence against that spouse or intimate partner, shall be punished as provided in subsection (b).

(b) Penalties. -

A person who violates this section or section 2261A shall be fined under this title, imprisoned -

(1)

for life or any term of years, if death of the victim results;

(2)

for not more than 20 years if permanent disfigurement or life threatening bodily injury to the victim results;

(3)

for not more than 10 years, if serious bodily injury to the victim results or if the offender uses a dangerous weapon during the offense;

(4)

as provided for the applicable conduct under chapter 109A if the offense would constitute an offense under chapter 109A (without regard to whether the offense was committed in the special maritime and territorial jurisdiction of the United States or in a Federal prison); and

(5)

for not more than 5 years, in any other case,

or both fined and imprisoned

Next

US CODE COLLECTION

search

Prev | Next

Sec. 2261A. - Interstate stalking

Whoever -

Search this title:

Search Title 18

Notes
Updates
Parallel authorities
(CFR)
Topical references

(1)

> travels in interstate or foreign commerce or within the special maritime and territorial jurisdiction of the United States, or enters or leaves Indian country, with the intent to kill, injure, harass, or intimidate another person, and in the course of, or as a result of, such travel places that person in reasonable fear of the death of, or serious bodily injury to, that person, a member of the immediate family (as defined in section 115) of that person, or the spouse or intimate partner of that person; or

(2)

> with the intent -

(A)

> to kill or injure a person in another State or tribal jurisdiction or within the special maritime and territorial jurisdiction of the United States; or

(B)

> to place a person in another State or tribal jurisdiction, or within the special maritime and territorial jurisdiction of the United States, in reasonable fear of the death of, or serious bodily injury to -

(i)

> that person;

(ii)

> a member of the immediate family (as defined in

section 115) of that person; or

(iii)

a spouse or intimate partner of that person, uses the mail or any facility of interstate or foreign commerce to engage in a course of conduct that places that person in reasonable fear of the death of, or serious bodily injury to, any of the persons described in clauses (i) through (iii), shall be punished as provided in section 2261(b)

Prev | Next

US CODE COLLECTION

TITLE 18 > PART I > CHAPTER 111 > Sec. 2280.

Prev | Next

Search this title:

Search Title 18

Notes
Updates
Parallel authorities
(CFR)
Topical references

Sec. 2280. - Violence against maritime navigation

(a) Offenses. -

(1) In general. -

A person who unlawfully and intentionally -

(A)

seizes or exercises control over a ship by force or threat thereof or any other form of intimidation;

(B)

performs an act of violence against a person on board a ship if that act is likely to endanger the safe navigation of that ship;

(C)

destroys a ship or causes damage to a ship or to its cargo which is likely to endanger the safe navigation of that ship;

(D)

places or causes to be placed on a ship, by any means whatsoever, a device or substance which is likely to destroy that ship, or cause damage to that ship or its cargo which endangers or is likely to endanger the safe navigation of that ship;

(E)

destroys or seriously damages maritime navigational facilities or seriously interferes with their operation, if such act is likely to endanger the safe navigation of a ship;

(F)

communicates information, knowing the information to be false and under circumstances in which such information may reasonably be believed, thereby endangering the safe navigation of a ship;

(G)

injures or kills any person in connection with the commission or the attempted commission of any of the offenses set forth in subparagraphs (A) through (F); or

(H)

attempts or conspires to do any act prohibited under subparagraphs (A) through (G),

shall be fined under this title, imprisoned not more than 20 years, or both; and if the death of any person results from conduct prohibited by this paragraph, shall be punished by death or imprisoned for any term of years or for life.

(2) Threat to navigation. -

A person who threatens to do any act prohibited under paragraph (1)(B), (C) or (E), with apparent determination and will to carry the threat into execution, if the threatened act is likely to endanger the safe navigation of the ship in question, shall be fined under this title, imprisoned not more than 5 years, or both.

(b) Jurisdiction. -

There is jurisdiction over the activity prohibited in subsection (a) -

(1)

in the case of a covered ship, if -

(A)

such activity is committed -

(i)

against or on board a ship flying the flag of the United States at the time the prohibited activity is committed;

(ii)

in the United States; or

(iii)

by a national of the United States or by a stateless person whose habitual residence is in the United States;

(B)

during the commission of such activity, a national of the United States is seized, threatened, injured or killed; or

(C)

the offender is later found in the United States after such activity is committed;

(2)

in the case of a ship navigating or scheduled to navigate solely within the territorial sea or internal waters of a country other than the United States, if the offender is later found in the United States after such activity is committed; and

(3)

in the case of any vessel, if such activity is committed in an attempt to compel the United States to do or abstain from doing any act.

(c) Bar To Prosecution. -

It is a bar to Federal prosecution under subsection (a) for conduct that occurred within the United States that the conduct involved was during or in relation to a labor dispute, and such conduct is prohibited as a felony under the law of the State in which it was committed. For purposes of this section, the term "labor dispute" has the meaning set forth in section 2(c) [1] of the Norris-LaGuardia Act, as amended (29 U.S.C. 113(c)). "13(c)".

(d) Delivery of Suspected Offender. -

The master of a covered ship flying the flag of the United States who has reasonable grounds to believe that there is on board that ship any person who has committed an offense under Article 3 of the Convention for the Suppression of Unlawful Acts Against the Safety of Maritime Navigation may deliver such person to the authorities of a State Party to that Convention. Before delivering such person to the authorities of another country, the master shall notify in an appropriate manner the Attorney General of the United States of the alleged offense and await instructions from the Attorney General as to what action to take. When delivering the person to a country which is a State Party to the Convention, the master shall, whenever practicable, and if possible before entering the territorial sea of such country, notify the authorities of such country of the master's intention to deliver such person and the reasons therefor. If the master delivers such person, the master shall furnish to the authorities of such country the evidence in the master's possession that pertains to the alleged offense.

(e) Definitions. -

In this section - "covered ship" means a ship that is navigating or is scheduled to navigate into, through or from waters beyond the outer limit of the territorial sea of a single country or a lateral limit of that country's territorial sea with an adjacent country. "national of the United States" has the meaning stated in section 101(a)(22) of the Immigration and Nationality Act (8 U.S.C. 1101(a)(22)). "territorial sea of the United States" means all waters extending seaward to 12 nautical miles from the baselines of the United States determined in accordance with international law. "ship" means a vessel of any type whatsoever not permanently attached to the sea-bed, including dynamically supported craft, submersibles or any other floating craft, but does not include a warship, a ship owned or operated by a government when being used as a naval auxiliary or for customs or police purposes, or a ship which has been withdrawn from navigation or laid up.

"United States", when used in a geographical sense, includes the Commonwealth of Puerto Rico, the Commonwealth of the Northern Mariana Islands and all territories and possessions of the United States

---

[1] So in original. Probably should be section

Prev | Next

US CODE COLLECTION

search

Prev

Sec. 2281. - Violence against maritime fixed platforms

(a) Offenses. -

   (1) In general. -

      A person who unlawfully and intentionally -

    (A)

       seizes or exercises control over a fixed platform by force or threat thereof or any other form of intimidation;

    (B)

       performs an act of violence against a person on board a fixed platform if that act is likely to endanger its safety;

    (C)

       destroys a fixed platform or causes damage to it which is likely to endanger its safety;

    (D)

       places or causes to be placed on a fixed platform, by any means whatsoever, a device or substance which is likely to destroy that fixed platform or likely to endanger its safety;

    (E)

       injures or kills any person in connection with the commission or the attempted commission of any of the offenses set forth in subparagraphs (A) through (D); or

    (F)

Search this title:

Search Title 18

Notes
Updates
Parallel authorities
(CFR)
Topical references

attempts or conspires to do anything prohibited under subparagraphs (A) through (E),

shall be fined under this title, imprisoned not more than 20 years, or both; and if death results to any person from conduct prohibited by this paragraph, shall be punished by death or imprisoned for any term of years or for life.

(2) Threat to safety. -

A person who threatens to do anything prohibited under paragraph (1)(B) or (C), with apparent determination and will to carry the threat into execution, if the threatened act is likely to endanger the safety of the fixed platform, shall be fined under this title, imprisoned not more than 5 years, or both.

(b) Jurisdiction. -

There is jurisdiction over the activity prohibited in subsection (a) if -

(1)

such activity is committed against or on board a fixed platform -

(A)

that is located on the continental shelf of the United States;

(B)

that is located on the continental shelf of another country, by a national of the United States or by a stateless person whose habitual residence is in the United States; or

(C)

in an attempt to compel the United States to do or abstain from doing any act;

(2)

during the commission of such activity against or on board a fixed platform located on a continental shelf, a national of the United States is seized, threatened, injured or killed; or

(3)

such activity is committed against or on board a fixed platform located outside the United States and beyond the continental shelf of the United States and the offender is later found in the United States.

(c) Bar To Prosecution. -

It is a bar to Federal prosecution under subsection (a) for conduct that occurred within the United States that the conduct involved was during or in relation to a labor dispute, and such conduct is prohibited as a felony under the law of the State in which it was committed. For purposes of this section, the term "labor dispute" has the meaning set forth in section 2(c) [1] of the Norris-LaGuardia Act, as amended (29 U.S.C. 113(c)), and the term "State" means a State of the United States, the District of Columbia, and any commonwealth, territory, or possession of the United States. "13(c)".

(d) Definitions. -

In this section - "continental shelf" means the sea-bed and subsoil of the submarine areas that extend beyond a country's territorial sea to the limits provided by customary international law as reflected in Article 76 of the 1982 Convention on the Law of the Sea. "fixed platform" means an artificial island, installation or structure permanently attached to the sea-bed for the purpose of exploration or exploitation of resources or for other economic purposes. "national of the United States" has the meaning stated in section 101(a)(22) of the Immigration and Nationality Act (8 U.S.C. 1101(a)(22)). "territorial sea of the United States" means all waters extending seaward to 12 nautical miles from the baselines of the United States determined in accordance with international law.

"United States", when used in a geographical sense, includes the Commonwealth of Puerto Rico, the Commonwealth of the Northern Mariana Islands and all territories and possessions of the United States

---

[1] So in original. Probably should be section

Prev

US CODE COLLECTION

TITLE 18 > PART I > CHAPTER 113B > Sec. 2332.

Prev | Next

Sec. 2332. - Criminal penalties

(a) Homicide. -

Whoever kills a national of the United States, while such national is outside the United States, shall -

(1)

if the killing is murder (as defined in section 1111 (a)), be fined under this title, punished by death or imprisonment for any term of years or for life, or both;

(2)

if the killing is a voluntary manslaughter as defined in section 1112(a) of this title, be fined under this title or imprisoned not more than ten years, or both; and

(3)

if the killing is an involuntary manslaughter as defined in section 1112(a) of this title, be fined under this title or imprisoned not more than three years, or both.

(b) Attempt or Conspiracy With Respect to Homicide. -

Whoever outside the United States attempts to kill, or engages in a conspiracy to kill, a national of the United States shall -

(1)

in the case of an attempt to commit a killing that is a murder as defined in this chapter, be fined under this title or imprisoned not more than 20 years, or both; and

(2)

in the case of a conspiracy by two or more persons to commit a killing that is a murder as defined in section

Search this title:

Search Title 18

Notes
Updates
Parallel authorities
(CFR)
Topical references

<u>1111</u>(a) of this title, if one or more of such persons do any overt act to effect the object of the conspiracy, be fined under this title or imprisoned for any term of years or for life, or both so fined and so imprisoned.

(c) Other Conduct. -

Whoever outside the United States engages in physical violence -

(1)

with intent to cause serious bodily injury to a national of the United States; or

(2)

with the result that serious bodily injury is caused to a national of the United States;

shall be fined under this title or imprisoned not more than ten years, or both.

(d) Limitation on Prosecution. -

No prosecution for any offense described in this section shall be undertaken by the United States except on written certification of the Attorney General or the highest ranking subordinate of the Attorney General with responsibility for criminal prosecutions that, in the judgment of the certifying official, such offense was intended to coerce, intimidate, or retaliate against a government or a civilian population.

Prev | Next

LII

legal information institute

collection home

search

TITLE 18 > PART I > CHAPTER 113B > Sec. 2332a.

Prev | Next

Search this title:

Search Title 18

Notes
Updates
Parallel authorities
(CFR)
Topical references

Sec. 2332a. - Use of certain weapons of mass destruction

(a) Offense Against a National of the United States or Within the United States. -

A person who, without lawful authority, uses, threatens, or attempts or conspires to use, a weapon of mass destruction (other than a chemical weapon as that term is defined in section 229F), including any biological agent, toxin, or vector (as those terms are defined in section 178) -

(1)

against a national of the United States while such national is outside of the United States;

(2)

against any person within the United States, and the results of such use affect interstate or foreign commerce or, in the case of a threat, attempt, or conspiracy, would have affected interstate or foreign commerce; or

(3)

against any property that is owned, leased or used by the United States or by any department or agency of the United States, whether the property is within or outside of the United States,

shall be imprisoned for any term of years or for life, and if death results, shall be punished by death or imprisoned for any term of years or for life.

(b) Offense by National of the United States Outside of the United States. -

Any national of the United States who, without lawful authority, uses, or threatens, attempts, or conspires to use, a weapon of mass destruction (other than a chemical weapon (as that term is defined in section 229F)) outside of the United States shall be imprisoned for any term of years or for life, and if death results, shall be punished by death, or by imprisonment for any term of years or for life.

(c) Definitions. -

For purposes of this section -

(1)

the term "national of the United States" has the meaning given in section 101(a)(22) of the Immigration and Nationality Act (8 U.S.C. 1101(a)(22)); and

(2)

the term "weapon of mass destruction" means -

(A)

any destructive device as defined in section 921 of this title;

(B)

any weapon that is designed or intended to cause death or serious bodily injury through the release, dissemination, or impact of toxic or poisonous chemicals, or their precursors;

(C)

any weapon involving a disease organism; or

(D)

any weapon that is designed to release radiation or radioactivity at a level dangerous to human life

US CODE COLLECTION

Search this title:

Search Title 18

Notes
Updates
Parallel authorities
(CFR)
Topical references

Sec. 2332b. - Acts of terrorism transcending national boundaries

(a) Prohibited Acts. -

(1) Offenses. -

Whoever, involving conduct transcending national boundaries and in a circumstance described in subsection (b) -

(A)

kills, kidnaps, maims, commits an assault resulting in serious bodily injury, or assaults with a dangerous weapon any person within the United States; or

(B)

creates a substantial risk of serious bodily injury to any other person by destroying or damaging any structure, conveyance, or other real or personal property within the United States or by attempting or conspiring to destroy or damage any structure, conveyance, or other real or personal property within the United States;

in violation of the laws of any State, or the United States, shall be punished as prescribed in subsection (c).

(2) Treatment of threats, attempts and conspiracies. -

Whoever threatens to commit an offense under paragraph (1), or attempts or conspires to do so, shall be punished under subsection (c).

(b) Jurisdictional Bases. -

(1) Circumstances. -

The circumstances referred to in subsection (a) are -

(A)

the mail or any facility of interstate or foreign commerce is used in furtherance of the offense;

(B)

the offense obstructs, delays, or affects interstate or foreign commerce, or would have so obstructed, delayed, or affected interstate or foreign commerce if the offense had been consummated;

(C)

the victim, or intended victim, is the United States Government, a member of the uniformed services, or any official, officer, employee, or agent of the legislative, executive, or judicial branches, or of any department or agency, of the United States;

(D)

the structure, conveyance, or other real or personal property is, in whole or in part, owned, possessed, or leased to the United States, or any department or agency of the United States;

(E)

the offense is committed in the territorial sea (including the airspace above and the seabed and subsoil below, and artificial islands and fixed structures erected thereon) of the United States; or

(F)

the offense is committed within the special maritime and territorial jurisdiction of the United States.

(2) Co-conspirators and accessories after the fact. -

Jurisdiction shall exist over all principals and co-conspirators of an offense under this section, and accessories after the fact to any offense under this section, if at least one of the circumstances described in subparagraphs (A) through (F) of paragraph (1) is applicable to at least one offender.

(c) Penalties. -

(1) Penalties. -

Whoever violates this section shall be punished -

(A)

for a killing, or if death results to any person from any other conduct prohibited by this section, by death, or by imprisonment for any term of years or for life;

(B)

for kidnapping, by imprisonment for any term of years or for life;

(C)

for maiming, by imprisonment for not more than 35 years;

(D)

for assault with a dangerous weapon or assault resulting in serious bodily injury, by imprisonment for not more than 30 years;

(E)

for destroying or damaging any structure, conveyance, or other real or personal property, by imprisonment for not more than 25 years;

(F)

for attempting or conspiring to commit an offense, for any term of years up to the maximum punishment that would have applied had the offense been completed; and

(G)

for threatening to commit an offense under this section, by imprisonment for not more than 10 years.

(2) Consecutive sentence. -

Notwithstanding any other provision of law, the court shall not place on probation any person convicted of a violation of this section; nor shall the term of imprisonment imposed under this section run concurrently with any other term of imprisonment.

(d) Proof Requirements. -

The following shall apply to prosecutions under this section:

(1) Knowledge. -

The prosecution is not required to prove knowledge by any defendant of a jurisdictional base alleged in the indictment.

(2) State law. -

In a prosecution under this section that is based upon the adoption of State law, only the elements of the offense under State law, and not any provisions pertaining to criminal procedure or evidence, are adopted.

(e) Extraterritorial Jurisdiction. -

There is extraterritorial Federal jurisdiction -

(1)

over any offense under subsection (a), including any threat, attempt, or conspiracy to commit such offense; and

(2)

over conduct which, under section 3, renders any person an accessory after the fact to an offense under subsection (a).

(f) Investigative Authority. -

In addition to any other investigative authority with respect to violations of this title, the Attorney General shall have primary investigative responsibility for all Federal crimes of terrorism, and any violation of section 351(e), 844 (e), 844(f)(1), 956(b), 1361, 1366(b), 1366(c), 1751(e), 2152, or 2156 of this title, and the Secretary of the Treasury shall assist the Attorney General at the request of the Attorney General. Nothing in this section shall be construed to interfere with the authority of the United States Secret Service under section 3056.

(g) Definitions. -

As used in this section -

(1)

the term "conduct transcending national boundaries" means conduct occurring outside of the United States in addition to the conduct occurring in the United States;

(2)

the term "facility of interstate or foreign commerce" has the meaning given that term in section 1958(b)(2);

(3)

the term "serious bodily injury" has the meaning given that term in section 1365(g)(3);

(4)

the term "territorial sea of the United States" means all waters extending seaward to 12 nautical miles from the baselines of the United States, determined in accordance with international law; and

(5)

the term "Federal crime of terrorism" means an offense that -

(A)

is calculated to influence or affect the conduct of government by intimidation or coercion, or to retaliate against government conduct; and

(B)

is a violation of -

(i)

section 32 (relating to destruction of aircraft or aircraft facilities), 37 (relating to violence at international airports), 81 (relating to arson within special maritime and territorial jurisdiction), 175 or 175b (relating to biological weapons), 229 (relating to chemical weapons), subsection (a), (b), (c), or (d) of section 351 (relating to congressional, cabinet, and Supreme Court assassination and kidnaping), 831 (relating to nuclear materials), 842 (m) or

(n)

(relating to plastic explosives), 844(f)(2) or

(3)

(relating to arson and bombing of Government property risking or causing death), 844(i) (relating to arson and bombing of property used in interstate commerce), 930(c) (relating to killing or attempted killing during an attack on a Federal facility with a dangerous weapon), 956(a)(1) (relating to conspiracy to murder, kidnap, or maim persons abroad), 1030(a)(1) (relating to protection of computers), 1030(a)(5)(A)(i) resulting in damage as defined in 1030(a)(5)(B)(ii) through

(v)

(relating to protection of computers), 1114 (relating to killing or attempted killing of officers and employees of the United States), 1116 (relating to murder or manslaughter of foreign officials, official guests, or internationally protected persons), 1203 (relating to hostage taking), 1362 (relating to destruction of communication lines, stations, or systems), 1363 (relating to injury to buildings or property within special maritime and territorial jurisdiction of the United States), 1366(a) (relating to destruction of an energy facility), 1751(a), (b), (c), or

(d)

(relating to Presidential and Presidential staff assassination and kidnaping), 1992 (relating to wrecking trains), 1993 (relating to terrorist attacks and other acts of violence against mass transportation systems), 2155 (relating to destruction of national defense materials, premises, or utilities), 2280 (relating to violence against maritime navigation), 2281 (relating to violence against maritime fixed platforms), 2332 (relating to certain homicides and other violence against United States nationals occurring outside of the United States), 2332a (relating to use of weapons of mass destruction), 2332b (relating to acts of terrorism transcending national boundaries), 2339 (relating to harboring terrorists), 2339A (relating to providing material support to terrorists), 2339B (relating to providing material support to terrorist organizations), or 2340A (relating to torture) of this title;

(ii)

section 236 (relating to sabotage of nuclear facilities or fuel) of the Atomic Energy Act of 1954 (42 U.S.C. 2284); or

(iii)

section 46502 (relating to aircraft piracy), the second sentence of section 46504 (relating to assault on a flight crew with a dangerous weapon), section 46505(b)(3) or (c) (relating to explosive or incendiary devices, or endangerment of human life by means of weapons, on aircraft), section 46506 if homicide or attempted homicide is involved (relating to application of certain criminal laws to acts on aircraft), or section 60123(b) (relating to destruction of interstate gas or hazardous liquid pipeline facility) of title 49

Prev | Next

US CODE COLLECTION

search

TITLE 18 > PART I > CHAPTER 113C > Sec. 2340A.

Prev | Next

Sec. 2340A. - Torture

(a) Offense. -

Whoever outside the United States commits or attempts to commit torture shall be fined under this title or imprisoned not more than 20 years, or both, and if death results to any person from conduct prohibited by this subsection, shall be punished by death or imprisoned for any term of years or for life.

(b) Jurisdiction. -

There is jurisdiction over the activity prohibited in subsection (a) if -

(1)

the alleged offender is a national of the United States; or

(2)

the alleged offender is present in the United States, irrespective of the nationality of the victim or alleged offender.

(c) Conspiracy. -

A person who conspires to commit an offense under this section shall be subject to the same penalties (other than the penalty of death) as the penalties prescribed for the offense, the commission of which was the object of the conspiracy.

Search this title:

Search Title 18

Notes
Updates
Parallel authorities (CFR)
Topical references

Prev | Next

© copyright   about us   send email

LII

legal information institute

collection home

US CODE COLLECTION

search

TITLE 18 > PART I > CHAPTER 118 > Sec. 2441.

Sec. 2441. - War crimes

(a) Offense. -

Whoever, whether inside or outside the United States, commits a war crime, in any of the circumstances described in subsection (b), shall be fined under this title or imprisoned for life or any term of years, or both, and if death results to the victim, shall also be subject to the penalty of death.

(b) Circumstances. -

The circumstances referred to in subsection (a) are that the person committing such war crime or the victim of such war crime is a member of the Armed Forces of the United States or a national of the United States (as defined in section 101 of the Immigration and Nationality Act).

(c) Definition. -

As used in this section the term "war crime" means any conduct -

(1)

defined as a grave breach in any of the international conventions signed at Geneva 12 August 1949, or any protocol to such convention to which the United States is a party;

(2)

prohibited by Article 23, 25, 27, or 28 of the Annex to the Hague Convention IV, Respecting the Laws and Customs of War on Land, signed 18 October 1907;

(3)

which constitutes a violation of common Article 3 of the international conventions signed at Geneva, 12

Search this title:

Search Title 18

Notes
Updates
Parallel authorities
(CFR)
Topical references

August 1949, or any protocol to such convention to which the United States is a party and which deals with non-international armed conflict; or

(4)

of a person who, in relation to an armed conflict and contrary to the provisions of the Protocol on Prohibitions or Restrictions on the Use of Mines, Booby-Traps and Other Devices as amended at Geneva on 3 May 1996 (Protocol II as amended on 3 May 1996), when the United States is a party to such Protocol, willfully kills or causes serious injury to civilians

CHAPTER FIVE   THE CONFLICT

These are my original notes I used to piece together what would become the only suit ever filed by an individual in the United States of America in an attempt to Repeal Roe v. Wade.

Can't have both

dumb, deaf, blind, disabled

always without a remedy — think!

1st Amendment

right

under the

Country

First

(to live)

II
III   XVI
IV   XVII
V   XVIII
VI   XIX
VII   XX
VIII   XXI
IX   XXII
X   XXIII
XI   XXIV
XII   XXV
XIII   XXVI
XIV
XV

Constitution

- guarantee life
- now recognized from conception
  Abortion is a [illegible] act
  without positive death

Rule of law #1111 & 1113
  [illegible] as dispute...
  a [illegible] act resolving death

unless [illegible] under the [illegible]

Abortion is guilty under this person

Violation of [illegible] of Unborn Children

Proclaiming innocent
- of death to death Organization law
But called to death — no rights to the Father

Moratorium

CHAPTER SIX   THE COMPLAINT

As you can see I painstakingly incorporated all the various protections afforded the human being in utero into the Complaint. Every spare moment I had since April 4th, 2004, night and day, was dedicated to compiling the research and putting together the Complaint.

I remember it was a beautiful April day when I went down to file the Federal Suit in the United States District Court for the Eastern District of Pennsylvania. The suit had to be reviewed first for accuracy, i.e., proper format, correct forms, etc. and all was found to be in order.

The suit was assigned to Federal Judge His Honor Robert F. Kelly, Sr. who would handle and rule on this case from beginning to end.

Fri Apr 16 13:45:35 358

UNITED STATES DISTRICT COURT

PHILADELPHIA , PA

Receipt No.   439 984109
Cashier   stevet

DC Code   Div No
4989   1

Sub Acct Type Type Tender   Amount
1:510200 N   )   90.00
2:086300 N   )   10.00

Total Amount $ 100.00

JOSEPH CATLIN

DOLLARS

UNITED STATES DISTRICT COURT FOR THE
EASTERN DISTRICT OF PENNSYLVANIA

Joseph E. Carlin 1137 E. Tioga Street 1st Floor Philadelphia, PA 19134 Plaintiff	: : :	CIVIL ACTION
v.	:	NO. 04-1666
United States of America C/O U.S. Department of Justice 950 Pennsylvania Avenue, NW Washington, DC 20530-0001 Defendant	: : : :	

COMPLAINT

TO THE HONORABLE, THE JUDGES OF THE SAID COURT:

Joseph E. Carlin, Plaintiff, brings forth this Complaint and avers as follows:

1. Joseph E. Carlin, Plaintiff, is a resident of 1137 E. Tioga Street, First Floor,

    Philadelphia, Pennsylvania 19134, and is a citizen of the United States of America.

2. Defendant, United States of America, is the Country of the United States of America,

    in perpetude, and is a citizen of the United States of America. Defendant's last

    known address is U.S. Department of Justice, 950 Pennsylvania Avenue, NW,

    Washington, DC 20530-0001.

3. This Honorable Court has jurisdiction to hear this Complaint.

DEFINITIONS

4. Plaintiff incorporates the averments made in paragraphs 1 through 3 as though fully

    contained herein.

Page 1 of 11

5. The Act means: H.R. 1997, One Hundred Eighth Congress of the United States of America, At The Second Session, An Act, To Amend Title 18, United States Code, and the Uniform Code of Military Justice to Protect Unborn Children From Assault, Murder and for other purposes. Also Known as the "Unborn Victims of Violence Act of 2004.

6. The Law means: Roe v. Wade, Decided January 22nd, 1973.

7. This Human Being means: A person, male or female, who is in utero

DISCUSSION

8. Plaintiff incorporates the averments made in paragraphs 1 through 7 as though fully contained herein.

9. The Act gives rights to this human being, protected under our Constitution and Title 18, United States Code, from the moment of conception.

10. The Act gives a voice to this human being who has no voice.

11. The Act recognizes life from the moment of conception and this human being, as being recognized as a person under the laws and jurisdiction of the United States of America, enjoys all the rights of any citizen of the United States of America.

12. The Act protects this human being from death or injury resulting in Drive-By Shootings.

13. The Act protects this human being from death or injury resulting in Violence at International Airports.

14. The Act protects this human being from death or injury resulting in Animal Enterprise Terrorism.

15. The Act protects this human being from death or injury resulting in Assaulting, resisting, or impeding certain officers or employees.

16. The Act protects this human being from death or injury resulting in Protection of foreign officials, official guests, and internationally protected persons.

17. The Act protects this human being from death or injury resulting in Assaults within maritime and territorial jurisdiction.

18. The Act protects this human being from death or injury resulting in maiming within maritime and territorial jurisdiction.

19. The Act protects this human being from death or injury resulting in influencing, impeding, or retaliating against a Federal official by threatening or injuring a family member.

20. The Act protects this human being from death or injury resulting in prohibited activities.

21. The Act protects this human being from death or injury resulting in deprivation of rights under color of law.

22. The Act protects this human being from death or injury resulting in Federally protected activities.

23. The Act protects this human being from death or injury resulting in damage to religious property; obstruction of persons in the free exercise of religious beliefs.

24. The Act protects this human being from death or injury resulting in freedom of access to clinic entrances.

25. The Act protects this human being from death or injury resulting in Congressional, Cabinet, and Supreme Court assassination, kidnapping, and assualt.

26. The Act protects this human being from death or injury resulting in prohibited transactions involving nuclear materials.

27. The Act protects this human being from death or injury resulting in any explosive materials.

28. The Act protects this human being from death or injury resulting in imports or possession of firearms or ammunition illegally.

29. The Act protects this human being from death or injury resulting in possession of firearms and dangerous weapons in Federal facilities.

30. The Act protects this human being from death or injury resulting in murder.

31. The Act protects this human being from death or injury resulting in manslaughter.

32. The Act protects this human being from death or injury resulting in attempting to commit murder or manslaughter.

33. The Act protects this human being from death or injury resulting in protection of officers and employees of the United States.

34. The Act protects this human being from death or injury resulting in murder or manslaughter of foreign officials, official guests, or internationally protected persons.

35. The Act protects this human being from death or injury resulting in murder by a Federal prisoner.

36. The Act protects this human being from death or injury resulting in foreign murder of United States nationals.

37. The Act protects this human being from death or injury resulting in murder by escaped prisoners.

38. The Act protects this human being from death or injury resulting in killing persons aiding Federal investigations or State correctional officers.

39. The Act protects this human being from death or injury resulting in offenses committed within Indian country.

40. The Act protects this human being from death or injury resulting in kidnapping.

41. The Act protects this human being from death or injury resulting in hostage taking.

42. The Act protects this human being from death or injury resulting in tampering with consumer products.

43. The Act protects this human being from death or injury resulting in assault on process servers.

44. The Act protects this human being from death or injury resulting in influencing or injuring officer or juror generally.

45. The Act protects this human being from death or injury resulting in obstruction of proceedings before departments, agencies, and committees.

46. The Act protects this human being from death or injury resulting in tampering with a witness, victim, or an imformant.

47. The Act protects this human being from death or injury resulting in retaliating against a witness, victim, or an informant.

48. The Act protects this human being from death or injury resulting in Presidential and Presidential staff assassination, kidnapping, and assault.

49. The Act protects this human being from death or injury resulting in hazardous or injurious devices on Federal lands.

50. The Act protects this human being from death or injury resulting in interference with commerce by threats or violence.

51. The Act protects this human being from death or injury resulting in Interstate and foreign travel or transportation in aid of racketeering enterprises.

52. The Act protects this human being from death or injury resulting in use of interstate commerce facilities in the commission of murder-for-hire.

53. The Act protects this human being from death or injury resulting in violent crimes in aid of racketeering activity.

54. The Act protects this human being from death or injury resulting in bank robbery and incidental crimes.

55. The Act protects this human being from death or injury resulting in mail, money, or other property of the United States.

56. The Act protects this human being from death or injury resulting in Railway or steamboat post offices.

57. The Act protects this human being from death or injury resulting in robberies and burglaries involving controlled substances.

58. The Act protects this human being from death or injury resulting in motor vehicles.

59. The Act protects this human being from death or injury resulting in cruelty to seamen.

60. The Act protects this human being from death or injury resulting in assault or resistance.

61. The Act protects this human being from death or injury resulting in aggravated sexual abuse.

62. The Act protects this human being from death or injury resulting in sexual abuse resulting in death.

63. The Act protects this human being from death or injury resulting in Interstate domestic violence.

64. The Act protects this human being from death or injury resulting in Interstate stalking.

65. The Act protects this human being from death or injury resulting in violence against maritime navigation.

66. The Act protects this human being from death or injury resulting in violence against maritime fixed platforms.

67. The Act protects this human being from death or injury resulting in killing of United States nationals while outside the United States.

68. The Act protects this human being from death or injury resulting in use of certain weapons of mass destruction.

69. The Act protects this human being from death or injury resulting in acts of terrorism transcending national boundaries.

70. The Act protects this human being from death or injury resulting in torture.

71. The Act protects this human being from death or injury resulting in war crimes.

COUNT I – THE ACT

REPEAL OF SECTION (c) (1)

72. Plaintiff incorporates the averments made in paragraphs 1 through 71 as though fully contained herein.

73. Section (c)(1) of The Act is in direct contradiction with The Act itself and violates the rights recognized by this human being under the Constitution of the United States of America in that this section violates the general welfare of this human being and strips this human being of his/her rights under the Constitution of the United States of America, namely Amendments I through XXVII.

74. The Act recognizes this human being's rights to life from the moment of conception and is a contradiction unto itself in that it violates the rights of this human being while Section (c) (1) is permitted to remain part of The Act.

COUNT II – THE LAW

REPEAL OF ROE V. WADE

75. Plaintiff incorporates the averments made in paragraphs 1 through 74 as though fully contained herein.

76. The Act supersedes The Law in that The Act recognizes this human being's rights afforded to every American Citizen, now and from the moment of conception.

77. The Law is now a violation of this human being's rights afforded to him/her under the entire Constitution of the United States of America and must now be repealed.

CONCLUSION

78. Plaintiff incorporates the averments made in paragraphs 1 through 77 as though fully contained herein.

79. The Act, Section 248 – Freedom of access to clinic entrances, prohibits the death or injury of this human being outside a clinic, but permits the ultimate death of this human being while inside an abortion clinic.

80. The Act is in contradiction to itself and Section (c) (1) of The Act must be repealed.

81. The Act protects all the rights of this human being except while being put to death at an abortion clinic.

82. The Act defines murder as "…unlawful killing of a human being…deliberate…" which is exactly what happens to this human being at an abortion clinic.

83. The Act defines manslaughter as "…a lawful act which might produce death." In The Act itself, Section (1) states "…any person for the conduct relating to an abortion…". The Act is in contradiction to itself in that is defines a penalty for "…lawful…death…" but then permits abortion to exist which violates this human being's rights afforded him/her under The Act and the Constitution of the United States of America.

84. Abortion produces death to this human being who, under this act, has been guaranteed every right, protection and liberty the United States of America affords

85. every citizen who was not only born in this Country, but under this Act, who is now conceived in this Country.

86. The Act recognizes the rights of this human being from the moment of conception.

87. The Act also provides for an attempt to commit murder or manslaughter as a violation to this human being's rights.

88. The Act recognizes this human being's right to life.

89. The Act gives a voice to those human beings whom are voiceless, namely the unborn, but also recognizes the rights afforded them as is to every American under the Constitution of the United States of America.

90. Although there are many Americans who are voiceless, i.e., comatose, speechless, disabled to the point of taking care of themselves by and through direct verbal communication, they still enjoy every provision of protection afforded to this human being under this Act, however, without the provision of Section (c)(1) being repealed, this human being will never be permitted to enjoy all the other provisions of protection afforded these other Americans while abortion is still The Law.

91. The Act is a contradiction to itself and violates the rights of this human being to life, liberty and the pursuit of happiness while Section (c)(1) is in effect.

92. The Law even goes so far as to recognize the rights of this human being in one of the closing Articles 1195 in that ..."Whoever shall during parturition of the mother destroy the vitality or life in a child in a state of being born and before actual birth, which child would otherwise have been born alive...".

W H E R E F O R E, Plaintiff prays this Honorable Court will repeal Section (c)(1) of The Act and Repeal The Law, Roe v. Wade entirely.

_____   4-16-04
Joseph E. Carlin   Date

VERIFICATION

I, Joseph E. Carlin, the captioned Plaintiff in the above action, verify that the statements made in the foregoing document are true and correct to the best of my knowledge, information and belief. I understand that false statements herein are made subject to the penalties of 18 Pa. C.S. Section 4904, relating to unsworn falsification to authorities.

DATE: 4·16-04

Joseph E. Carlin

UNITED STATES DISTRICT COURT FOR THE
EASTERN DISTRICT OF PENNSYLVANIA

Joseph E. Carlin	:	CIVIL ACTION
1137 E. Tioga Street		
1st Floor	:	
Philadelphia, PA 19134		
Plaintiff	:	
v.	:	NO.
United States of America	:	
C/O U.S. Department of Justice		
950 Pennsylvania Avenue, NW	:	
Washington, DC 20530-0001		
Defendant	:	

ORDER

AND NOW, this _____ day of _____, 2004, it is hereby ORDERED

that Section (c)(1) of H.R. 1997, also referred to as "Unborn Victims of Violence Act of

2004", is hereby repealed and is no longer a part of any Law of the United States of

America.

_____
                                                            J.

UNITED STATES DISTRICT COURT FOR THE
EASTERN DISTRICT OF PENNSYLVANIA

Joseph E. Carlin 1137 E. Tioga Street 1st Floor Philadelphia, PA 19134 Plaintiff	: : :	CIVIL ACTION
v.	:	NO.
United States of America C/O U.S. Department of Justice 950 Pennsylvania Avenue, NW Washington, DC 20530-0001 Defendant	: : :	

ORDER

AND NOW, this _____ day of _____, 2004, it is hereby ORDERED

that the law governing abortion known as Roe v. Wade, decided January 22nd, 1973 is

hereby repealed and is no longer a part of any Law of the United States of America.

_____
                                                  J.

CHAPTER SEVEN   THE SOLICITATION

I was not naïve enough to believe that although I was trying to fight the good fight I would not be up against United States Attorney's with decades of experience in the law. I was right, there were three assigned to the case.

So I went to work again, this time I worked the internet to gather as many contacts as I could to try to get no cost representation. Here is the list of all the contacts I made. No one was interested in taking on the case.

I remember I even spoke with someone from The Texas Justice League/Foundation, something like that, and they were involved with the real "Roe" who was going to file something to try to Repeal Roe v. Wade. When I was told they were going to wait until the "anniversary" to file their suit. . .it was heart wrenching. With approximately 1.3 million abortions in the United States of America each year I just didn't see what the hold up was.

In my opinion, the pro-life organizations did have what they needed to repeal Roe v. Wade. Why wait? It just didn't make sense. Here I am, a high school graduate, from trial and error over the years learned how to "speak the court's language" and I sunk my teeth in on this almost immediately after the Act became law.

MISSISSIPPI (MEMPHIS)

info@dunbarmonroe.com
tnicholson@tlnanicholson.com
john@law-inc.com
4/24
llatham@latham-burell.com
*wbs@tecinfo.com
firm@gunnandhicks.com
btvance@watervalley.net   R-NO
keithcarlton@bellsouth.net

ALABAMA (BIRMINGHAM)

jwhatley@whatleydrake.com
gwandk@hiwaay.net
cparkerson@deslaw.com
4/24
info@year-out.net

info@smithalspaugh.com
johnwaddell1@aol.com
jlsatty@wwisp.com
Thefirm@hillhillcarter.com
a.toddcarter@knology.net
jimmyj@mindspring.com
msharper@tallassee.net
jwtlaw@earthlink.net

LOUISIANA (NEW OR

fc@laborlawyers.com
jandry@andrylawfirm.com
contact@fpkc.com
info@kanner-law.com
4/24
*tthompson@watkinsludlam.c
RLowe@LSHAH.com
matters@shergarner.com
mriley@kennejr.com
manager@smclattorneys.com
* johnsharp@sharphenry.com
gemcy@bellsouth.net
info@steen-williamson.com

UTAH (SALT LAKE

markmcl@xmission.com
bud@scalleyreading.net
coleman@bucklandorton.co
4/24
darrell@bostwickprice.com
lightninglaw@yahoo.com
rranney@charter.net

5/3/04

ARKANSAS

clark@fec.net
richardoworsham@
worshamlawfirm.com
triallaw@ipa.net
info@yearganlawfirm.com
JimPat@daggettlaw.com
malmlaw@alltel.net
foglemanrogers@aol.com

KENTUCKY

atty@lcgandm.com
info@ackersonlegal.com
NJA322@aol.com
kryan@bglaw.com
hcastty@insight.bb.com
mbaker@bakerkriz.com
wksii@fuse.net
mad@naglelaw.com
dpierce@psslaw.com

Virginia

Kmoran@wranktkerbrewka.com
ccowan@cowanowen.com
~~cfolandboit@aol.com~~
btparker2@earthlink.net
schmieleri@sslawfirm.com
kccatty@windspring.com
deadlaw@verizon.net
Will403@aol.com
eichler.pn@hotmail.com
mealbers@r990.com

VERMONT

teustace@firmspf.com
lfisher@rwmalaw.com
webmaster@clearyshahi.com

CHICAGO SUN-TIMES
mcooks@sintimes.com

LA TIMES

letters@latimes.com

4/21   NEW YORK TIMES
        [illegible]@[illegible].com
        [illegible]
        [illegible]
        [illegible]@washpost.com
4/22   [illegible]
4/23   [illegible]
4/3   [illegible]
4/23   [illegible]@nbc.com

[illegible]   THE TAPE

4/21   ABC WORLD NEWS TONIGHT
        [illegible]
        [illegible]@[illegible]law.com
        [illegible]@[illegible].com
        [illegible]
        [illegible]
        [illegible]@[illegible].com
*   [illegible]@hotmail (note)
        [illegible]
        DAILY[illegible]world.com
        [illegible]@[illegible].com
        Barry@BarryDinatoia.com
        [illegible]@[illegible]

Los Angeles

        Johnson & Richardson
        310-836-[illegible]
        LUCAS [illegible]
info@sdsatt.com
taylor@[illegible].com
info@blockmanlaw.com
Ton@[illegible]law firm.com
info@gonzaleslaw.com
info@[illegible].com
[illegible]
info@cohos-Ayala.com
ton@tjjlaw.com
Contactus@[illegible]law.com
moreinfo@thecochranfirm.com

Sacramento's

the [illegible]
[illegible]@nrlc.org
[illegible] George [illegible]
4   [illegible] Adams

4/21 IX-INFO@[illegible].net
4/2   contactus@[illegible]trustee.com
        NEW YORK
        [illegible]@[illegible].com
4/29 [illegible]
4/30 info@[illegible].com
4/2   [illegible]
        [illegible]

Subj:	**Pro Se Lawsuit I filed**
Date:	4/20/04 8:27:23 AM Pacific Daylight Time
From:	CarliJos2
To:	marshalldennehey@mdwcg.com

Dear Sir or Madam,

    I filed suit in District Court for the Eastern District of Pennsylvania on 4/16/04. I am not a lawyer. The suit asks for the repeal of Section (c)(1) of The Unborn Victims of Violence Act of 2004 signed into law on 4/6/04 and the repeal of Roe v. Wade entirely. The Act contradicts itself and contradicts Roe v. Wade altogether. I am actively seeking pro bono representation in this matter. If you'd like to take a look-see at the suit, no obligation of course, I'll e-mail you a copy. You can also reach me directly at 215-768-5934.

    Thank you, Joe Carlin

CHAPTER EIGHT   THE RESPONSE

June 18th, 2004 The United States of America, through their counsel, filed their answer to my Complaint. It's what's not said in their response that's most interesting. This is a copy.

**IN THE UNITED STATES DISTRICT COURT
FOR THE EASTERN DISTRICT OF PENNSYLVANIA**

JOSEPH E. CARLIN,)
)
  Plaintiff,) Civil Action No. 04-1666–RK
)
v.)
)
THE UNITED STATES OF AMERICA,)
)
  Defendant.)
)

MEMORANDUM OF LAW IN SUPPORT OF
DEFENDANT'S MOTION TO DISMISS PLAINTIFF'S COMPLAINT

PRELIMINARY STATEMENT

On April 1, 2004, the President signed into law the Unborn Victims of Violence Act of

2004, (the "Act"), Pub. L. No. 108-212, to be codified at 18 U.S.C. § 1841 and 10 U.S.C. § 919a.

Pursuant to the Act, a person who engages in conduct in violation of certain laws and "thereby

causes the death of, or bodily injury . . . to, a child, who is in utero at the time the conduct takes

place, is guilty of a separate offense . . . ." 18 U.S.C. § 1841(a)(1); 10 U.S.C. § 919a(a)(1).

Under this law, a person may not be prosecuted for "conduct relating to an abortion." 18 U.S.C.

§ 1841(c)(1); 10 U.S.C. § 919a(c)(1) ("section (c)(1)").

Plaintiff has filed a two-count complaint against the United States of America, requesting

(in count I) that section (c)(1) of the Act be "repealed" because, according to plaintiff, that

section is in "direct contradiction with The Act itself." Complaint at ¶ 73; see also id. at ¶¶ 80;

91. Plaintiff also requests (in count II) that the Court "repeal" Roe v. Wade because "The Act

recognizes this human being's rights afforded to every American Citizen, now and from the moment of conception." Complaint at ¶ 76; see also id. at ¶ 86 & p. 11.

Plaintiff's complaint should be dismissed for two main reasons. First, plaintiff lacks standing to bring his complaint. Instead of alleging a personal injury, plaintiff appears to have a general grievance about what the Act does not proscribe. But as is well-established by Supreme Court precedent, moral or policy objections to legislative acts do not confer Article III standing. Second, even if plaintiff had standing, his complaint still would be subject to dismissal for failure to state a claim upon which relief can be granted because he has not, and cannot, point to anything improper that Congress did in enacting section (c)(1). Moreover, in requesting that the Court strike down Roe v. Wade, plaintiff has requested that the Court reach beyond its authority and void Supreme Court precedent, which it cannot do.

As set forth more fully below, this Court should dismiss plaintiff's complaint.

STANDARDS

Rule 12(b)(1) of the Federal Rules of Civil Procedure allows a court to dismiss a claim for lack of subject matter jurisdiction. Where, as here, a challenge to a court's subject matter jurisdiction is made pursuant to Rule 12(b)(1), it is the burden of the party seeking to invoke the power of the court to establish that the relevant jurisdictional requirements are satisfied. See, e.g., Gould Elec., Inc. v. United States, 220 F.3d 169, 178 (3d Cir. 2000) (pursuant to Rule 12(b)(1), "[t]he plaintiff has the burden of persuasion to convince the court it has jurisdiction."); Development Fin. Corp. v. Alpha Hous. & Health Care, Inc., 54 F.3d 156, 158 (3d Cir.1995) (same).

Rule 12(b)(6) of the Federal Rules of Civil Procedure allows a court to dismiss an action for failure to state a claim upon which relief can be granted. In considering a Rule 12(b)(6) motion, the court "must accept all well pleaded factual allegations as true and draw all reasonable inferences from such allegations in favor of the complainant." Worldcom, Inc. v. Graphnet, Inc., 343 F.3d 651, 653 (3d Cir. 2003). Dismissal for failure to state a claim is appropriate only if it "appears beyond doubt that plaintiff can prove no set of facts in support of his claim which would entitle him to relief." Conley v. Gibson, 355 U.S. 41, 45-46 (1957).

ARGUMENT

I. PLAINTIFF LACKS STANDING TO MAINTAIN THIS ACTION.

"Article III, § 2, of the Constitution extends the 'judicial Power' of the United States only to 'Cases' and 'Controversies.'" Steel Co. v. Citizens for a Better Env't, 523 U.S. 83, 102 (1998). "In essence the question of standing is whether the litigant is entitled to have the court decide the merits of the dispute or of particular issues." Warth v. Seldin, 422 U.S. 490, 498 (1975). Standing "has a core component derived directly from the Constitution," and in order to meet the standing requirement of Article III, "[a] plaintiff must allege personal injury fairly traceable to the defendant's allegedly unlawful conduct and likely to be redressed by the requested relief." Allen v. Wright, 468 U.S. 737, 751 (1984). "The Court will not pass upon the validity of a statute upon complaint of one who fails to show that he is injured by its operation." Ashwander v. Tennessee Valley Auth., 297 U.S. 288, 346 (1936) (Brandeis, J., concurring).

In order to establish Article III standing, the Supreme Court has "consistently stressed that a plaintiff's complaint must establish that he has a 'personal stake' in the alleged dispute, and that the alleged injury suffered is particularized as to him." Raines v. Byrd, 521 U.S. 811, 819 (1997); see also Valley Forge Christian Coll. v. Americans United for Separation of Church & State, Inc., 454 U.S. 464, 472 (1982) ("Art. III requires the party who invokes the court's

- 3 -

authority to 'show that he personally has suffered some actual or threatened injury as a result of the putatively illegal conduct of the defendant.'") (citation omitted). "Abstract injury is not enough. The plaintiff must show that he 'has sustained or is immediately in danger of sustaining some direct injury' as the result of the challenged official conduct and the injury or threat of injury must be both 'real and immediate,' not 'conjectural' or 'hypothetical.'" City of Los Angeles v. Lyons, 461 U.S. 95, 101-02 (1983) (citations omitted).

Plaintiff has failed to establish that he has suffered a personal or concrete Article III injury. At most, Mr. Carlin's injury is that he does not approve of the exception contained in the Unborn Victims of Violence Act of 2004. Such an injury, based on dissatisfaction with government conduct, however, is not personal or concrete, and it does not confer standing. See Lujan v. Defenders of Wildlife, 504 U.S. 555, 573-74 (1992) ("We have consistently held that a plaintiff raising only a generally available grievance about government – claiming only harm to his and every citizen's interest in proper application of the Constitution and laws, and seeking relief that no more directly and tangibly benefits him than it does the public at large – does not state an Article III case or controversy."); Diamond v. Charles, 476 U.S. 54, 65 (1986) (Physician-litigant lacked standing because the physician's effort to maintain the litigation was "simply an effort to compel the State to enact a code in accord with the [physician's] interests" and "the power to create and enforce a legal code . . . is one of the quintessential functions of a State.") (internal quotations and citation omitted).

Federal courts are not the proper forum to air grievances such as the one alleged by plaintiff. He has alleged only that he does not approve of section (c)(1), but he has not alleged how he has been personally injured by that provision. Plaintiff plainly has failed to establish that he, himself, has an Article III injury. In the absence of any constitutionally meaningful injury, he does not have standing to lodge his complaint.

II. PLAINTIFF'S COMPLAINT DOES NOT SET FORTH A CLAIM UPON WHICH RELIEF CAN BE GRANTED.

Even if this Court were to find that plaintiff has suffered an injury-in-fact and has standing to challenge the Act, his complaint still should be dismissed. Plaintiff alleges that the Act improperly prohibits prosecution for conduct relating to abortion, and requests that the provision that disallows such prosecution be stricken. Complaint at ¶¶ 72-74. These are not claims upon which relief can be granted.

In enacting section (c)(1), Congress acted within the bounds of its legislative authority. Plaintiff has failed to allege anything that Congress did improperly in enacting the Unborn Victims of Violence Act of 2004, requiring, or even authorizing, this Court to strike down any of its provisions. Count I of plaintiff's complaint, accordingly, should be dismissed pursuant to Federal Rule of Civil Procedure 12(b)(6). Moreover, this Court does not have authority to overturn a decision by the Supreme Court, and, therefore, Count II of plaintiff's Complaint, seeking the repeal of Roe v. Wade, likewise, should be dismissed.

CONCLUSION

For the foregoing reasons, plaintiff's complaint should be dismissed for lack of subject matter jurisdiction or for failure to state a claim upon which relief can be granted.

Dated: June 18, 2004

Respectfully submitted,

PETER D. KEISLER
Assistant Attorney General

PATRICK L. MEEHAN
United States Attorney

ANTHONY J. COPPOLINO
Special Litigation Counsel

/s/ Kaija M. Clark
KAIJA M. CLARK (D.C. Bar No. 467376)
Trial Attorney
United States Department of Justice
20 Massachusetts Ave., N.W., Rm. 7126
Washington, D.C. 20530
Tel.: (202) 514-3489; Fax: (202) 616-8470
Kaija.Clark@usdoj.gov

**IN THE UNITED STATES DISTRICT COURT
FOR THE EASTERN DISTRICT OF PENNSYLVANIA**

JOSEPH E. CARLIN,	)	
	)	Civil Action No. 04-1666–RK
Plaintiff,	)	
v.	)	
	)	
THE UNITED STATES OF AMERICA,	)	
	)	
Defendant.	)	

PROPOSED ORDER

Upon consideration of Defendant's Motion to Dismiss Plaintiff's Complaint, it is hereby

ORDERED that Defendant's Motion to Dismiss Plaintiff's Complaint is GRANTED, and it is

FURTHER ORDERED that Plaintiff's Complaint is DISMISSED.

SO ORDERED.

Date: _____, 2004   By: _____
                                          United States District Judge

**IN THE UNITED STATES DISTRICT COURT
FOR THE EASTERN DISTRICT OF PENNSYLVANIA**

JOSEPH E. CARLIN,	: CIVIL ACTION
Plaintiff,	:
v.	: NO. 04-1666
UNITED STATES OF AMERICA,	:
Defendant.	:

ROBERT F. KELLY, Sr. J.   **JULY 26, 2004**

MEMORANDUM

Presently pending before this Court is the Motion to Dismiss of Defendant United

States of America ("United States"). For the following reasons, the United States' Motion will

be granted.

I. BACKGROUND

Joseph E. Carlin ("Carlin") filed a *pro se* Complaint against the United States on

April 16, 2004. The two-Count Complaint revolves around the Unborn Victims of Violence Act

of 2004 (the "Act"). 18 U.S.C. § 1841; 10 U.S.C. § 919a. The Act provides that any person who

violates certain laws and "thereby causes the death of, or bodily injury . . . to, a child, who is in

utero at the time the conduct takes place, is guilty of a separate offense. . . ." 18 U.S.C. §

1841(a)(1); 10 U.S.C. § 919a(a)(1). Significantly, for purposes of this case, the Act excludes

prosecution "for conduct relating to an abortion for which the consent of the pregnant woman, or

a person authorized by law to act on her behalf, has been obtained or for which such consent is

implied by law." ("Section (c)(1)"). 18 U.S.C. § 1841(c)(1); 10 U.S.C. § 919a(c)(1).

As previously mentioned, Carlin raises two Counts in his Complaint. In Count I, Carlin requests that this Court repeal Section (c)(1) based on the claim that this provision is allegedly in "direct contradiction with The Act itself." Moreover, in Count II of his Complaint, Carlin asks this Court to repeal the United States Supreme Court's decision in Roe v. Wade based on the contention that the Act allegedly supersedes this case. 410 U.S. 113 (1973). The United States filed the instant Motion for Dismiss on June 18, 2004. The United States argues that this action is appropriate for dismissal pursuant to Rules 12(b)(1)[1] and 12(b)(6) of the Federal Rules of Civil Procedure. Carlin filed a Response to the present Motion on June 24, 2004.

II. STANDARD OF REVIEW

Carlin has filed a *pro se* action in this Court. As an initial matter, on a motion to dismiss, the district court must construe a *pro se* plaintiff's allegations liberally and apply a less stringent standard to the pleadings of a *pro se* plaintiff than to a complaint prepared by an attorney. Haines v. Kerner, 404 U.S. 519, 520-21 (1972).

"Challenges to plaintiff's standing to sue are jurisdictional and are considered under Rule 12(b)(1)." In re Walnut Leasing Co., Inc., No. 99-526, 1999 WL 729267, at *1 (E.D. Pa. Sept. 8, 1999). Rule 12(b)(1) permits a court to dismiss an action for lack of subject matter jurisdiction. FED. R. CIV. P. 12(b)(1). "[F]or purposes of ruling on a motion to dismiss for want for standing . . . 'the trial court . . . must accept as true all allegations of the complaint, and must construe the complaint in favor of the complaining party.'" McGrath v. Johnson, 67 F. Supp.2d

---

[1] The United States' argument pursuant to Rule 12(b)(1) is that this Court lacks subject matter jurisdiction based on the contention that Carlin lacks standing to pursue his claims in this Court.

499, 505 (E.D. Pa. 1999)(quoting Warth v. Seldin, 422 U.S. 490, 501 (1975)).

III. DISCUSSION

The United States has moved to dismiss Carlin's Complaint for lack of subject matter jurisdiction pursuant to Rule 12(b)(1) and failure to state a claim upon which relief can be granted under Rule 12(b)(6). This Court agrees with the United States' argument that Carlin lacks standing to pursue his claims in federal court. Thus, dismissal of the action is appropriate under Rule 12(b)(1). This Court finds it unnecessary to address the United States' Rule 12(b)(6) argument because dismissal is appropriate on the alternative ground.

The jurisdictional reach of the federal courts extends only to "cases" and "controversies" pursuant to Article III of the United States Constitution. U.S. CONST. art. III, § 2; Allen v. Wright, 468 U.S. 737, 750 (1984). In order to establish standing in a federal court "[a] plaintiff must allege personal injury fairly traceable to the defendant's allegedly unlawful conduct and likely to be redressed by the requested relief." Allen, 468 U.S. at 751. In the area of standing, the United States Supreme Court "has consistently stressed that a plaintiff's complaint must establish that he has a 'personal stake' in the alleged dispute, that the alleged injury suffered is particularized as to him." Raines v. Byrd, 521 U.S. 811, 819 (1997). Finally, it is well established that an "abstract injury" or "generalized grievance" is insufficient to meet the requisite standing requirements. Streater v. U.S. Dep't of Transp., No. 95-2162, 1996 WL 134807, at *4 (E.D. Pa. Mar. 25, 1996).

In this case, Carlin has not alleged that he has suffered any particularized personal injury in relation to the claims in his Complaint. In essence, through his Complaint, Carlin simply voices his disapproval of Section (c)(1) of the Act and offers his own viewpoint on the

3

Act's impact on United States Supreme Court precedent. These general grievances and opinions relating to the Act and its influence on the law are insufficient to establish standing in this Court. Streater, 1996 WL 134807, at *4. Carlin has failed to allege any personal injury related to the allegations in his Complaint that would give him standing to continue with his claims in this Court. Thus, Carlin's Complaint must be dismissed pursuant to Rule 12(b)(1) because the jurisdictional requirement of standing is lacking in this case.

IV. CONCLUSION

For the reasons set forth above, this Court finds that Carlin lacks standing to proceed with his claims in this Court. Thus, dismissal of Carlin's claims is appropriate pursuant to Rule 12(b)(1).

An appropriate Order follows.

**IN THE UNITED STATES DISTRICT COURT
FOR THE EASTERN DISTRICT OF PENNSYLVANIA**

JOSEPH E. CARLIN,	:	CIVIL ACTION
Plaintiff,	:	
v.	:	NO. 04-1666
UNITED STATES OF AMERICA,	:	
Defendant.	:	

ORDER

AND NOW, this 26th day of July, 2004, upon consideration of the Defendant's

Motion to Dismiss (Doc. No. 4), and the Plaintiff's Response thereto, it is hereby **ORDERED**

that the Motion is **GRANTED** and the case is **DISMISSED WITH PREJUDICE**. The Clerk

of Court is hereby directed to mark this case as closed.

BY THE COURT:_____

_____Robert F. Kelly,   Sr. J.

CHAPTER NINE   MY FOLLOW-UP RESPONSE

I wasted no time in my reply. On June 23rd, 2004 I filed my answer to their response.   I think you can see I felt they were skirting the issue. This is a copy of my follow-up response.

IN THE UNITED STATES DISTRICT COURT
FOR THE EASTERN DISTRICT OF PENNSYLVANIA

Joseph E. Carlin Plaintiff	:	
	:	CIVIL ACTION
v.	:	NO. 04-1666-RK
United States of America Defendant	:	

Addressed to:

Eastern District of Pennsylvania
Office of Clerk
United States District Court
Philadelphia, PA 19106-1797

Please file the within Plaintiff's Response to Defendant's Motion to Dismiss and Memorandum of Law in Support of Defendant's Motion to Dismiss Plaintiff's Complaint in the above captioned matter.

Date: 6/23/04

Joseph E. Carlin

IN THE UNITED STATES DISTRICT COURT
FOR THE EASTERN DISTRICT OF PENNSYLVANIA

Joseph E. Carlin   :
Plaintiff

                      :   CIVIL ACTION

v.   :   NO. 04-1666-RK

United States of America :
Defendant

PLAINTIFF'S RESPONSE TO DEFENDANT'S MOTION
TO DISMISS AND MEMORANDUM OF LAW IN SUPPORT OF
DEFENDANT'S MOTION TO DISMISS PLAINTIFF'S COMPLAINT

TO THE HONORABLE, THE JUDGES OF THE SAID COURT:

Plaintiff incorporates the above captioned Complaint as though fully contained

herein and answers/avers as follows:

DEFENDANT'S SUBHEADING "PRELIMINARY STATEMENT"

1. Paragraph 1: Accepted.

2. Paragraph 2: Accepted.

3. Paragraph 3: Accepted in part, denied in part. Plaintiff does have standing to bring

forth this Complaint. Plaintiff finds controversy within the Act. The Act

contradicts itself in that this human being's rights to protection from harm under Title 18

(Manslaughter) are being violated thereby contradicting the Act itself and ultimately the

Law. Moral and policy objections to legislative acts do confer standing as those objections are the right of every Citizen, including those covered under the umbrella of the Act, and are within the jurisdictional boundaries of this Honorable Court to enforce.

Defendant even goes as far as to imply that Plaintiff does have standing. Congress made a mistake in enacting Section (c)(1) of the Act., be it unintentionally, which gave rise to Plaintiff's Complaint.

4. Paragraph 4: Denied.

DEFENDANT'S SUBHEADING "STANDARDS"

5. Paragraph 1: Accepted in part, denied in part. The Federal Rules of Civil Procedure also permits a Court (This Honorable Court) to sustain a claim. This human being's rights are being violated within the jurisdiction of This Honorable Court and therefore this Court has satisfied any relevant jurisdictional requirements to make a ruling in this matter. This Honorable Court, within its relevant jurisdiction, has the right and duty to offer the protections Title 18 provided to every Citizen within its jurisdiction, even to those human beings now given the same rights as every other Citizen under the Act.

6. Paragraph 2: Accepted.

DEFENDANT'S SUBHEADING "ARGUMENT" (I)

7. Paragraph 1: Accepted in part, denied in part.

8. Paragraph 2: Accepted.

9. Paragraph 3: Accepted. Defendant acknowledges that "the power to create...legal code...is one of the quintessential functions of a State."

10. Paragraph 4: Denied.

DEFENDANT'S SUBHEADING "ARGUMENT" (II)

11. Paragraph 1: Accepted in part, denied in part. Defendant acknowledges that This Honorable Court can find in favor of Plaintiff's Complaint. The relief requested in the Complaint can be granted by This Honorable Court. The Act is flawed. The Law violates protections offered by the Act.

12. Paragraph 2: Accepted in part, denied in part. This Honorable Court can make a Ruling based on the protections offered under Title 18, now being violated by the Act and the Law, to all persons within this Honorable Courts' jurisdiction.

DEFENDANT'S SUBHEADING "CONCLUSION"

13. Paragraph 1: Denied.

PLAINTIFF'S ARGUMENT TO SUSTAIN PLAINTIFF'S COMPLAINT AND DISMISS DEFENDANT'S MOTION TO DISMISS PLAINTIFF'S COMPLAINT

14. Plaintiff incorporates the answers and averments made in paragraphs 1 through 13 as though fully contained herein.

15. The United States Constitution clearly states…"We the People of the United States, in Order to form a more perfect Union, establish Justice, insure domestic tranquility, provide for the common defense, promote the general welfare, and secure the Blessings of Liberty to ourselves and our Posterity, do ordain and establish this Constitution for the United States of America."

16. Article III Section 1 of the Constitution clearly states…"The Judicial Power of the United States, shall be vested in one Supreme Court, and in such inferior Courts as the

Congress from time to time ordain and establish." Defendant is attempting to circumvent this Honorable Court's Judicial Power by:

(a) suggesting this Honorable Court has no Judicial Power to provide for the common defense of Citizens, including those now covered under the Act, within its jurisdictional boundaries.

(b) suggesting this Honorable Court has no Judicial Power to provide domestic tranquility to the Citizens, including those now covered under the Act, within its jurisdictional boundaries.

(c) suggesting this Honorable Court has no Judicial Power to promote the general welfare of Citizens, including those now covered under the Act, within its jurisdictional boundaries.

(d) suggesting this Honorable Court has no Judicial Power to secure the Blessings of Liberty to ourselves and our Posterity to the Citizens, including those now covered under the Act, within its jurisdictional boundaries.

17. Article III Section 2 of the Constitution was referenced by Defendant wherein Defendant stated…"Standing"…has a core component derived directly from the Constitution,"…although this core component may have been referenced in the past concerning a personal injury case, the key word here is "derived".

18. Webster's Dictionary defines "derived" as: to take, receive or obtain especially from a specified source.

19. The "specified source" as referenced by the Defendant is the United States Constitution. The rest is left up to interpretation.

20. Plaintiff's interpretation of this matter, including standing and jurisdictional authority, differ from those of Defendant.

21. Plaintiff derives from Article III Section 2 that..."Judicial Power shall extend to...controversies to which the United States shall be a party..."

22. Plaintiff believes, and therefore avers, that a controversy lies within the Act which in turn affects the Law.

23. Plaintiff is a Citizen of the United States of America and has standing to bring this controversy to be judged by this Honorable Court, this Judicial Power.

24. This Honorable Court, as a Judicial Power, has jurisdiction to bring this matter to trial.

25. Plaintiff is required, as per the Defendant, to not only establish standing but jurisdictional authority as well. Plaintiff believes this has been accomplished.

26. In quoting President Woodrow Wilson, "Liberty has never come from government. The history of liberty is the history of limitations of government's power, not the increase of it." In sustaining Plaintiff's Complaint this Honorable Court will be taking an enormous step in securing the "Blessings of Liberty" guaranteed every Citizen of the United States of America, being the same liberties now guaranteed those human beings covered under the Act.

W H E R E F O R E, Plaintiff prays this Honorable Court will DENY Defendant's Motion to Dismiss Plaintiff's Complaint and sustain Plaintiff's Complaint and GRANT the relief requested.

_____   _____
Joseph E. Carlin, Pro Se   Date

IN THE UNITED STATES DISTRICT COURT
FOR THE EASTERN DISTRICT OF PENNSYLVANIA

Joseph E. Carlin   :
Plaintiff

                         :   CIVIL ACTION

v.   :   NO. 04-1666-RK

United States of America   :
Defendant

VERIFICATION

I, Joseph E. Carlin, the captioned Plaintiff in the above action, verify that the statements made in the foregoing document are true and correct to the best of my knowledge, information and belief. I understand that false statements herein are made subject to penalties of 18 Pa. C.S. Section 4904, relating to unsworn falsification to authorities.

DATE: _6-23-04_

                                       Joseph E. Carlin

IN THE UNITED STATES DISTRICT COURT
FOR THE EASTERN DISTRICT OF PENNSYLVANIA

Joseph E. Carlin Plaintiff	:	
	:	CIVIL ACTION
v.	:	NO. 04-1666-RK
United States of America Defendant	:	

ORDER

AND NOW, This _____ day of _____, 2004, Upon

consideration of Defendant's Motion To Dismiss Plaintiff's Complaint and Memorandum

of Law in Support of Defendant's Motion to Dismiss Plaintiff's Complaint and Plaintiff's

Response thereto, it is hereby ORDERED that Defendant's Motion to Dismiss Plaintiff's

Complaint is DENIED.

_____
United States District Judge

IN THE UNITED STATES DISTRICT COURT
FOR THE EASTERN DISTRICT OF PENNSYLVANIA

Joseph E. Carlin   :
Plaintiff

                   :   CIVIL ACTION

v.   :   NO. 04-1666-RK

United States of America   :
Defendant

CERTIFICATE OF SERVICE

I, Joseph E. Carlin, the captioned Plaintiff in the above action, verify that a true and correct copy of the Plaintiff's Response To Defendant's Motion To Dismiss And Memorandum Of Law In Support Of Defendant's Motion To Dismiss Plaintiff's Complaint was served upon the Defendant in the following manner:

By First Class Mail addressed to

Kaija M. Clark, Esquire
Trial Attorney
United States Department of Justice
20 Massachusetts Avenue, N.W.
Room 7126
Washington, D.C. 20530

DATE: _0-23-04_
                                     Joseph E. Carlin

IN THE UNITED STATES DISTRICT COURT
FOR THE EASTERN DISTRICT OF PENNSYLVANIA

JOSEPH E. CARLIN,)	
)	Civil Action No. 04-1666–RK
Plaintiff,)	
v.)	
)	
THE UNITED STATES OF AMERICA,)	
)	
Defendant.)	

MEMORANDUM OF LAW IN SUPPORT OF
DEFENDANT'S MOTION TO DISMISS PLAINTIFF'S COMPLAINT

PRELIMINARY STATEMENT

On April 1, 2004, the President signed into law the Unborn Victims of Violence Act of

2004, (the "Act"), Pub. L. No. 108-212, to be codified at 18 U.S.C. § 1841 and 10 U.S.C. § 919a.

Pursuant to the Act, a person who engages in conduct in violation of certain laws and "thereby

causes the death of, or bodily injury . . . to, a child, who is in utero at the time the conduct takes

place, is guilty of a separate offense . . . ." 18 U.S.C. § 1841(a)(1); 10 U.S.C. § 919a(a)(1).

Under this law, a person may not be prosecuted for "conduct relating to an abortion." 18 U.S.C.

§ 1841(c)(1); 10 U.S.C. § 919a(c)(1) ("section (c)(1)").

Plaintiff has filed a two-count complaint against the United States of America, requesting

(in count I) that section (c)(1) of the Act be "repealed" because, according to plaintiff, that

section is in "direct contradiction with The Act itself." Complaint at ¶ 73; see also id. at ¶¶ 80;

91. Plaintiff also requests (in count II) that the Court "repeal" Roe v. Wade because "The Act

recognizes this human being's rights afforded to every American Citizen, now and from the moment of conception." Complaint at ¶ 76; see also id. at ¶ 86 & p. 11.

Plaintiff's complaint should be dismissed for two main reasons. First, plaintiff lacks standing to bring his complaint. Instead of alleging a personal injury, plaintiff appears to have a general grievance about what the Act does not proscribe. But as is well-established by Supreme Court precedent, moral or policy objections to legislative acts do not confer Article III standing. Second, even if plaintiff had standing, his complaint still would be subject to dismissal for failure to state a claim upon which relief can be granted because he has not, and cannot, point to anything improper that Congress did in enacting section (c)(1). Moreover, in requesting that the Court strike down Roe v. Wade, plaintiff has requested that the Court reach beyond its authority and void Supreme Court precedent, which it cannot do.

As set forth more fully below, this Court should dismiss plaintiff's complaint.

STANDARDS

Rule 12(b)(1) of the Federal Rules of Civil Procedure allows a court to dismiss a claim for lack of subject matter jurisdiction. Where, as here, a challenge to a court's subject matter jurisdiction is made pursuant to Rule 12(b)(1), it is the burden of the party seeking to invoke the power of the court to establish that the relevant jurisdictional requirements are satisfied. See, e.g., Gould Elec., Inc. v. United States, 220 F.3d 169, 178 (3d Cir. 2000) (pursuant to Rule 12(b)(1), "[t]he plaintiff has the burden of persuasion to convince the court it has jurisdiction."); Development Fin. Corp. v. Alpha Hous. & Health Care, Inc., 54 F.3d 156, 158 (3d Cir.1995) (same).

Rule 12(b)(6) of the Federal Rules of Civil Procedure allows a court to dismiss an action for failure to state a claim upon which relief can be granted. In considering a Rule 12(b)(6) motion, the court "must accept all well pleaded factual allegations as true and draw all reasonable inferences from such allegations in favor of the complainant." Worldcom, Inc. v. Graphnet, Inc., 343 F.3d 651, 653 (3d Cir. 2003). Dismissal for failure to state a claim is appropriate only if it "appears beyond doubt that plaintiff can prove no set of facts in support of his claim which would entitle him to relief." Conley v. Gibson, 355 U.S. 41, 45-46 (1957).

ARGUMENT

I. PLAINTIFF LACKS STANDING TO MAINTAIN THIS ACTION.

"Article III, § 2, of the Constitution extends the 'judicial Power' of the United States only to 'Cases' and 'Controversies.'" Steel Co. v. Citizens for a Better Env't, 523 U.S. 83, 102 (1998). "In essence the question of standing is whether the litigant is entitled to have the court decide the merits of the dispute or of particular issues." Warth v. Seldin, 422 U.S. 490, 498 (1975). Standing "has a core component derived directly from the Constitution," and in order to meet the standing requirement of Article III, "[a] plaintiff must allege personal injury fairly traceable to the defendant's allegedly unlawful conduct and likely to be redressed by the requested relief." Allen v. Wright, 468 U.S. 737, 751 (1984). "The Court will not pass upon the validity of a statute upon complaint of one who fails to show that he is injured by its operation." Ashwander v. Tennessee Valley Auth., 297 U.S. 288, 346 (1936) (Brandeis, J., concurring).

In order to establish Article III standing, the Supreme Court has "consistently stressed that a plaintiff's complaint must establish that he has a 'personal stake' in the alleged dispute, and that the alleged injury suffered is particularized as to him." Raines v. Byrd, 521 U.S. 811, 819 (1997); see also Valley Forge Christian Coll. v. Americans United for Separation of Church & State, Inc., 454 U.S. 464, 472 (1982) ("Art. III requires the party who invokes the court's

- 3 -

authority to 'show that he personally has suffered some actual or threatened injury as a result of the putatively illegal conduct of the defendant.'") (citation omitted). "Abstract injury is not enough. The plaintiff must show that he 'has sustained or is immediately in danger of sustaining some direct injury' as the result of the challenged official conduct and the injury or threat of injury must be both 'real and immediate,' not 'conjectural' or 'hypothetical.'" City of Los Angeles v. Lyons, 461 U.S. 95, 101-02 (1983) (citations omitted).

Plaintiff has failed to establish that he has suffered a personal or concrete Article III injury. At most, Mr. Carlin's injury is that he does not approve of the exception contained in the Unborn Victims of Violence Act of 2004. Such an injury, based on dissatisfaction with government conduct, however, is not personal or concrete, and it does not confer standing. See Lujan v. Defenders of Wildlife, 504 U.S. 555, 573-74 (1992) ("We have consistently held that a plaintiff raising only a generally available grievance about government — claiming only harm to his and every citizen's interest in proper application of the Constitution and laws, and seeking relief that no more directly and tangibly benefits him than it does the public at large — does not state an Article III case or controversy."); Diamond v. Charles, 476 U.S. 54, 65 (1986) (Physician-litigant lacked standing because the physician's effort to maintain the litigation was "simply an effort to compel the State to enact a code in accord with the [physician's] interests" and "the power to create and enforce a legal code . . . is one of the quintessential functions of a State.") (internal quotations and citation omitted).

Federal courts are not the proper forum to air grievances such as the one alleged by plaintiff. He has alleged only that he does not approve of section (c)(1), but he has not alleged how he has been personally injured by that provision. Plaintiff plainly has failed to establish that he, himself, has an Article III injury. In the absence of any constitutionally meaningful injury, he does not have standing to lodge his complaint.

II.   PLAINTIFF'S COMPLAINT DOES NOT SET FORTH A CLAIM UPON WHICH RELIEF CAN BE GRANTED.

Even if this Court were to find that plaintiff has suffered an injury-in-fact and has standing to challenge the Act, his complaint still should be dismissed. Plaintiff alleges that the Act improperly prohibits prosecution for conduct relating to abortion, and requests that the provision that disallows such prosecution be stricken. Complaint at ¶¶ 72-74. These are not claims upon which relief can be granted.

In enacting section (c)(1), Congress acted within the bounds of its legislative authority. Plaintiff has failed to allege anything that Congress did improperly in enacting the Unborn Victims of Violence Act of 2004, requiring, or even authorizing, this Court to strike down any of its provisions. Count I of plaintiff's complaint, accordingly, should be dismissed pursuant to Federal Rule of Civil Procedure 12(b)(6). Moreover, this Court does not have authority to overturn a decision by the Supreme Court, and, therefore, Count II of plaintiff's Complaint, seeking the repeal of Roe v. Wade, likewise, should be dismissed.

CONCLUSION

For the foregoing reasons, plaintiff's complaint should be dismissed for lack of subject matter jurisdiction or for failure to state a claim upon which relief can be granted.

Dated: June 18, 2004

Respectfully submitted.

PETER D. KEISLER
Assistant Attorney General

PATRICK L. MEEHAN
United States Attorney

ANTHONY J. COPPOLINO
Special Litigation Counsel

/s/ Kaija M. Clark
KAIJA M. CLARK (D.C. Bar No. 467376)
Trial Attorney
United States Department of Justice
20 Massachusetts Ave., N.W., Rm. 7126
Washington, D.C. 20530
Tel.: (202) 514-3489; Fax: (202) 616-8470
Kaija.Clark@usdoj.gov

IN THE UNITED STATES DISTRICT COURT
FOR THE EASTERN DISTRICT OF PENNSYLVANIA

JOSEPH E. CARLIN,   )
)
)   Civil Action No. 04-1666-RK
            Plaintiff,   )
v.   )
)
THE UNITED STATES OF AMERICA,   )
)
            Defendant.   )
)

PROPOSED ORDER

Upon consideration of Defendant's Motion to Dismiss Plaintiff's Complaint, it is hereby

ORDERED that Defendant's Motion to Dismiss Plaintiff's Complaint is GRANTED, and it is

FURTHER ORDERED that Plaintiff's Complaint is DISMISSED.

SO ORDERED.

Date: _____, 2004   By: _____

                                          United States District Judge

CHAPTER TEN   THE ORDER

No standing. . .personally injured. . .what the Order does not say is the most interesting part. His Honor, in Section II, Standard of Review, noted ". . .for purposes of ruling on a motion to dismiss for want of standing. . .'the trial court. . . must accept as true all allegations of the complaint, and must construe the complaint in favor of the complaining party."

Section II speaks for itself. The allegations I made in my Complaint are accepted as true.

The case was "dismissed with prejudice" which means I am barred from re-filing the case again, but, due to the ways and the means in how the case was dismissed, it still can be referenced by another party due to the acceptance of my allegations as truth.

I am not a lawyer, I have had no formal training, I can only call them as I see them and that's why I know, after all these years of silence, I know I can dedicate myself to the Repeal of Roe v. Wade and see it through.

**IN THE UNITED STATES DISTRICT COURT
FOR THE EASTERN DISTRICT OF PENNSYLVANIA**

JOSEPH E. CARLIN,	:	CIVIL ACTION
	:	
Plaintiff,	:	
	:	
v.	:	NO. 04-1666
	:	
UNITED STATES OF AMERICA,	:	
	:	
Defendant.	:	

ROBERT F. KELLY, Sr. J.   **JULY 26, 2004**

MEMORANDUM

Presently pending before this Court is the Motion to Dismiss of Defendant United States of America ("United States"). For the following reasons, the United States' Motion will be granted.

I. BACKGROUND

Joseph E. Carlin ("Carlin") filed a *pro se* Complaint against the United States on April 16, 2004. The two-Count Complaint revolves around the Unborn Victims of Violence Act of 2004 (the "Act"). 18 U.S.C. § 1841; 10 U.S.C. § 919a. The Act provides that any person who violates certain laws and "thereby causes the death of, or bodily injury . . . to, a child, who is in utero at the time the conduct takes place, is guilty of a separate offense. . . ." 18 U.S.C. § 1841(a)(1); 10 U.S.C. § 919a(a)(1). Significantly, for purposes of this case, the Act excludes prosecution "for conduct relating to an abortion for which the consent of the pregnant woman, or a person authorized by law to act on her behalf, has been obtained or for which such consent is implied by law." ("Section (c)(1)"). 18 U.S.C. § 1841(c)(1); 10 U.S.C. § 919a(c)(1).

As previously mentioned, Carlin raises two Counts in his Complaint. In Count I, Carlin requests that this Court repeal Section (c)(1) based on the claim that this provision is allegedly in "direct contradiction with The Act itself." Moreover, in Count II of his Complaint, Carlin asks this Court to repeal the United States Supreme Court's decision in Roe v. Wade based on the contention that the Act allegedly supersedes this case. 410 U.S. 113 (1973). The United States filed the instant Motion for Dismiss on June 18, 2004. The United States argues that this action is appropriate for dismissal pursuant to Rules 12(b)(1)[1] and 12(b)(6) of the Federal Rules of Civil Procedure. Carlin filed a Response to the present Motion on June 24, 2004.

II. STANDARD OF REVIEW

Carlin has filed a *pro se* action in this Court. As an initial matter, on a motion to dismiss, the district court must construe a *pro se* plaintiff's allegations liberally and apply a less stringent standard to the pleadings of a *pro se* plaintiff than to a complaint prepared by an attorney. Haines v. Kerner, 404 U.S. 519, 520-21 (1972).

"Challenges to plaintiff's standing to sue are jurisdictional and are considered under Rule 12(b)(1)." In re Walnut Leasing Co., Inc., No. 99-526, 1999 WL 729267, at *1 (E.D. Pa. Sept. 8, 1999). Rule 12(b)(1) permits a court to dismiss an action for lack of subject matter jurisdiction. FED. R. CIV. P. 12(b)(1). "[F]or purposes of ruling on a motion to dismiss for want for standing . . . 'the trial court . . . must accept as true all allegations of the complaint, and must construe the complaint in favor of the complaining party.'" McGrath v. Johnson, 67 F. Supp.2d

---

[1] The United States' argument pursuant to Rule 12(b)(1) is that this Court lacks subject matter jurisdiction based on the contention that Carlin lacks standing to pursue his claims in this Court.

499, 505 (E.D. Pa. 1999)(quoting Warth v. Seldin, 422 U.S. 490, 501 (1975)).

III. DISCUSSION

The United States has moved to dismiss Carlin's Complaint for lack of subject matter jurisdiction pursuant to Rule 12(b)(1) and failure to state a claim upon which relief can be granted under Rule 12(b)(6). This Court agrees with the United States' argument that Carlin lacks standing to pursue his claims in federal court. Thus, dismissal of the action is appropriate under Rule 12(b)(1). This Court finds it unnecessary to address the United States' Rule 12(b)(6) argument because dismissal is appropriate on the alternative ground.

The jurisdictional reach of the federal courts extends only to "cases" and "controversies" pursuant to Article III of the United States Constitution. U.S. CONST. art. III, § 2; Allen v. Wright, 468 U.S. 737, 750 (1984). In order to establish standing in a federal court "[a] plaintiff must allege personal injury fairly traceable to the defendant's allegedly unlawful conduct and likely to be redressed by the requested relief." Allen, 468 U.S. at 751. In the area of standing, the United States Supreme Court "has consistently stressed that a plaintiff's complaint must establish that he has a 'personal stake' in the alleged dispute, that the alleged injury suffered is particularized as to him." Raines v. Byrd, 521 U.S. 811, 819 (1997). Finally, it is well established that an "abstract injury" or "generalized grievance" is insufficient to meet the requisite standing requirements. Streater v. U.S. Dep't of Transp., No. 95-2162, 1996 WL 134807, at *4 (E.D. Pa. Mar. 25, 1996).

In this case, Carlin has not alleged that he has suffered any particularized personal injury in relation to the claims in his Complaint. In essence, through his Complaint, Carlin simply voices his disapproval of Section (c)(1) of the Act and offers his own viewpoint on the

Act's impact on United States Supreme Court precedent. These general grievances and opinions relating to the Act and its influence on the law are insufficient to establish standing in this Court. Streater, 1996 WL 134807, at *4. Carlin has failed to allege any personal injury related to the allegations in his Complaint that would give him standing to continue with his claims in this Court. Thus, Carlin's Complaint must be dismissed pursuant to Rule 12(b)(1) because the jurisdictional requirement of standing is lacking in this case.

IV. CONCLUSION

For the reasons set forth above, this Court finds that Carlin lacks standing to proceed with his claims in this Court. Thus, dismissal of Carlin's claims is appropriate pursuant to Rule 12(b)(1).

An appropriate Order follows.

IN THE UNITED STATES DISTRICT COURT
FOR THE EASTERN DISTRICT OF PENNSYLVANIA

JOSEPH E. CARLIN,	CIVIL ACTION
Plaintiff,	
v.	NO. 04-1666
UNITED STATES OF AMERICA,	
Defendant.	

ORDER

AND NOW, this 26th day of July, 2004, upon consideration of the Defendant's

Motion to Dismiss (Doc. No. 4), and the Plaintiff's Response thereto, it is hereby **ORDERED**

that the Motion is **GRANTED** and the case is **DISMISSED WITH PREJUDICE**. The Clerk

of Court is hereby directed to mark this case as closed.

BY THE COURT:_____

_____Robert F. Kelly,   Sr. J.

CHAPTER ELEVEN   WHAT IS STANDING?

I would have to show I was injured somehow as a result of the Act and the Law. I couldn't do that and that was never an issue in my Complaint, but, it was something the United States Attorney's zeroed in on and exploited versus confronting the true issues of the Complaint.

It took three United States Attorneys over two months to come up with that strategy.

Well, this is why this case can get expensive. What I need to do is find:

A woman who had an abortion who was not aware of the Unborn Victims of Violence Act.

The woman would need to be either injured physically or mentally (or both) as a result of the abortion.

The woman would need to offer testimony that if in fact she had known about the Unborn Victims of Violence Act (and the provisions therein that life begins at the moment of conception and the human being in utero had rights identical to hers) that she would have never had an abortion.

That woman is out there. I know it.

CHAPTER TWELVE   THE LIQUORIAN

Some two years later I attended Mass (once again by chance) at Immaculate Conception BVM Church in Jenkintown, PA. There was a guest speaker, Father Quinn, who was the editor of The Liquorian, a Catholic pro-life periodical.

I met with Father Quinn after Mass and told him about what I tried to do a couple years ago. He was interested in taking a look at the suit and I sent him a copy.

He ran it by some of his people and they agreed with His Honor, I had no standing to bring the suit.

What I said to him was, there certainly had to be someone out there that did have standing, that the groundwork had already been laid out on this case, if his periodical could help find that one person a new case could be filed along the same lines with someone who does have standing.

Joseph E. Carlin
456 Tyson Avenue
Glenside, PA 19038
215-768-5934

October 17, 2006

Father Quinn
800 East Lancaster Avenue
St. Thomas Monastery
Villanova, PA 19085

Dear Father,

We met briefly Sunday after 11:30 Mass at Immaculate Conception. Enclosed is a copy of the suit I filed in an attempt to have Roe v. Wade repealed. I filed this ten days after the Unborn Victims of Violence Act became law. I felt it gave "teeth" to a suit to have Roe repealed but no one took up this issue in Court, so I did. I tried anyway.

Father, I'm nothing special. I'm not a lawyer. I'm not a college grad. I'm just a kid from Kensington who graduated from North Catholic.

I told my children this is the sixth greatest thing I did in my life. I have five children.

Would you please give me a call and let me know you are in receipt of this package.

Thanks again,

Joseph E. Carlin

CHAPTER THIRTEEN   FINAL THOUGHTS AND THANKS

In 2010 I directed and produced a feature length film. During that time I met a man who wanted to help promote the film. It was through this man that I learned his wife was arrested thirty times for protesting at abortion clinics. I met her and told her she was my new hero.

I had personal issues publicizing this case because I refused to benefit from what was happening to these little victims. I think meeting this woman was a way to let me know that I not only had to get this case filed again but if I were going to dedicate my time and effort to get this done I also had to be able to survive.

A large portion of proceeds I make on this book will go to fund the enormous legal fees it will take to get this case back in front of a Federal Judge and ultimately the United States Supreme Court. I've made this book as inexpensively as possible and very, very affordable. Rest assured, when you purchase this book you are contributing to the Repeal of Roe v. Wade.

I've always thought this battle to Repeal Roe v. Wade, although helped with prayers and peaceful protest, would be done through the courts where it all became law.

If a woman can get a government paid for abortion then why can't the same woman get government paid for birth control, at any age, at any time, no questions asked. That should go for men as well, at any age, at any time, no questions asked.

Through the intercession of the recently Beautified Pope John Paul II this effort will result in the Repeal of Roe v. Wade. Thank you.

The full Docket appears here as well.

CLOSED, SPECIAL

United States District Court
Eastern District of Pennsylvania (Philadelphia)
CIVIL DOCKET FOR CASE #: 2:04-cv-01666-RK

CARLIN v. UNITED STATES OF AMERICA
Assigned to: HONORABLE ROBERT F. KELLY
Cause: 42:1983 Civil Rights Act

Date Filed: 04/16/2004
Date Terminated: 07/26/2004
Jury Demand: None
Nature of Suit: 440 Civil Rights: Other
Jurisdiction: U.S. Government
Defendant

Plaintiff

JOSEPH E. CARLIN   represented by **JOSEPH E. CARLIN**
1137 E. TIOGA STREET
1ST FLOOR
PHILA.,, PA 19134
PRO SE

V.

Defendant

UNITED STATES OF AMERICA   represented by **KAIJA M. CLARK**
DEPARTMENT OF JUSTICE
20 MASSACHUSETTS AVE NW
RM 7126
CIVIL DIVISION
WASHINGTON, DC 20530
202-514-3489
Email: KAIJA.CLARK@USDOJ.GOV
ATTORNEY TO BE NOTICED

Date Filed	#	Docket Text
04/16/2004	1	COMPLAINT against UNITED STATES OF AMERICA (Filing fee $ 150 receipt number 904108.), filed by JOSEPH E. CARLIN.(cw,) (mk,). (Entered: 04/16/2004)
04/16/2004		Summons Issued as to UNITED STATES OF AMERICA, One Given to U.S. Attorney and Two Forwarded To: Pro Se on 04/16/04 (cw,) (Entered: 04/16/2004)
04/16/2004		Disclosure Statement by JOSEPH E. CARLIN.(cw,) (Entered: 04/16/2004)
04/19/2004	2	Acceptance of Service by U.S. Attorney re: accepted summons and complaint for UNITED STATES OF AMERICA on 4/19/2004, answer due 6/18/2004. (mbh,) (mk,). (Entered: 04/19/2004)

04/26/2004	3	SUMMONS Returned Executed as to USA re: served DEFENDANT UNITED STATES OF AMERICA by Certified Mail Return Receipt Requested on 4/22/2004, answer due 6/21/2004. (mbh,) (Entered: 04/26/2004)
06/18/2004	4	MOTION to Dismiss for Lack of Jurisdiction filed by UNITED STATES OF AMERICA., Certificate of Service. (Attachments: # 1 Exhibit Memorandum in Support of Motion# 2 Text of Proposed Order)(CLARK, KAIJA) Modified on 6/21/2004 (fh) (Entered: 06/18/2004)
06/24/2004	5	RESPONSE to Defendant's Motion to Dismiss and Memorandum of Law in Support of Defendant's Motion to Dismiss Plaintiff's Complaint filed by JOSEPH E. CARLIN. Certificate of Service (stb,) (mk,). (Entered: 06/24/2004)
07/26/2004	6	MEMORANDUM AND ORDER THAT DEFENDANT'S MOTION TO DISMISS IS GRANTED AND THE CASE IS DISMISSED WITH PREJUDICE. THE CLERK OF COURT IS DIRECTED TO MARK THIS CASE CLOSED. SIGNED BY JUDGE ROBERT F. KELLY ON 7/26/2004. 7/26/2004 ENTERED AND COPIES MAILED.(mbh,) (Entered: 07/26/2004)

PACER Service Center			
Transaction Receipt			
05/30/2011 11:36:26			
PACER Login:	jc5022	Client Code:	
Description:	Docket Report	Search Criteria:	2:04-cv-01666-RK
Billable Pages:	2	Cost:	0.16

END NOTES

Copyright is claimed on my written words and thoughts, not on any public record or public domain items.

Research is printed herein with permission from Cornell University.

At the time of printing this book, Patrick Meehan, one of the United States Attorneys, is now a United States Congressman.

A large portion of every sale will go towards legal fees to re-file a case using the Unborn Victims of Violence Act as the anchor to establish human beings conceived in America and in utero have the same rights as those human beings who were conceived in America and are out of utero.

I know what type of law firm I want to take this case, and in a nut shell, they will be expensive.

This is about the issue of contradiction between the Law and the Act. The Law will be repealed.